David McGill's
COMPLETE
kiwi slanG
DICTIONARY

To James,

So you won't
feel like a stranger
in a "strange"
land!!

Liz & Alec

REED

Published by Reed Books, a division of Reed Publishing (NZ) Ltd, 39 Rawene Rd, Birkenhead, Auckland. Associated companies, branches and representatives throughout the world.

ISBN 0 7900 0595 6

© 1998 David McGill text
© 1998 Kevin Wildman illustrations

The author and illustrator assert their moral rights in the work.

First published 1998

Printed in New Zealand

Introduction

This collection of slang and Kiwi catchphrases is as comprehensive and contemporary as I can make something so quick-moving and ephemeral as the informal language of New Zealanders.

I began collecting Kiwi slang in London in 1968, when I found irresistible the phrases of a New Zealand flatmate, Brett, who first startled me with language as exuberant as any Barry Humphries was using in his Bazza McKenzie strip cartoon of the time. My first recorded slang-note was in my 1968 diary, Brett assuring me that if something was not so then 'my arse is a red cabbage'. I have been collecting ever since.

This book is based on my 1988, 1989 and 1995 published collections of Kiwi slang. The first collection was tutored by my English lecturer of the early 1960s, Kiwi lexicographer extraordinaire Harry Orsman, who has compiled the *Heinemann New Zealand Dictionary*, 1979; with Jan Moore the *Heinemann Dictionary of New Zealand Quotations*, 1988; the *New Zealand Slang Dictionary* and *The Beaut Little Book of New Zealand Slang*, Reed, 1992; with Elizabeth Orsman *The New Zealand Dictionary*, New House Publishers, 1994; in 1997 his magnum opus, *The Oxford Dictionary of New Zealand English*.

I have extended Kiwi slang from the solitary predecessor to my 1988 collection, Sidney Baker's *New Zealand Slang, A Dictionary of Colloquialisms*, Whitcombe and Tombs, 1941. I have attempted to sift out Kiwi slang from the flood of comparative Australian, American, English and Canadian collections of slang, and also from the hybrid *A Personal Kiwi-Yankee Dictionary* by Louis S. Leland Jnr., 1980. It is as easy a task as identifying the origins of individual grains of sand on a beach.

The only slang that is unquestionably uniquely Kiwi is the mix and muddle of Maori and English, the likes of 'electric puha' and 'up the boohai'. My arbiters in the many grey areas have often been two internationally renowned lexicographers who happen to be New Zealanders, Eric Partridge with the bible of slang books, *A Dictionary of Slang and Unconventional English*, which I also first encountered in London in 1968, and Robert Burchfield, editor of the *Oxford English Dictionary Supplement*. Also of help were George Turner with *The English Language in Australia and New Zealand*, Longmans, 1966, J.A.W. Bennett for 'English As It Is Spoken in New Zealand' in *English Transported*, Australian University Press, Canberra, 1970, and my former professor of English at Victoria University of Wellington, Scotsman Ian Gordon, editor of *The New Collins Concise English Dictionary New Zealand Edition*, 1982.

New Zealand writers and social commentators have yielded much slang, including Jim Henderson, Gordon Slatter, Keri Hulme, Noel Hilliard, Stevan Eldred-Grigg, Frank S. Anthony, Barry Crump, Edward Jerningham Wakefield, John A. Lee, Charles Money, Tom Scott, C.R. Thatcher, Lady Barker, Roger Hall, Alison Gray, Alex Veysey, Judith Fyfe and Hugo Manson, Burton Silver, Ruth Mason, Peter Cape, L.G.D. Acland, David Burton, A.S. Thomson, Arnold Wall, Jim and Mary Barr, Gordon McLauchlan, Peter Mahon, Frank Haden, Bill Pearson, J. Magurk, John McDermott, Austin Mitchell, A.W. Reed, Herbert W. Williams. I am grateful to television, radio, the press and magazines, most particularly sports commentators like Keith Quinn, Stu Wilson and Graham Lowe, and the indefatigable Paul Holmes and enthusiastic Jim Hickey, for many examples of Kiwi slang.

I am grateful to those who have written or rung or confronted me with contributions, including Roger Steele, Bun and Monk Shepherd, Ian Forsyth, M. Fletcher, Charles Johnstone, Bob Hancock, Nigel Watson, Tony Burton, Jo Mildenhall, Grant Tilly, Tracey Williams, N.A. Rigden, N. Butt, L.J. Nielson, M. Malmanche, Erena Josling, Greg Peacocke, L. Hyslop, G. Hurdle, M. Hiddlestone, N. Frew, A. Dick, J. White, M. Geddes, R. Newton, K.J. Davis, C. Hampson, C. Corbett, David V. Coy, R.M. Cairns, Mrs Spinner, C. Johnstone, F.C. Smith, M. Rodwell, M. Burnside, G., P., R. and K. McDonald, Kay Barraclough, R.L. Jackman, G. Clark, G. Hall, M.B. Taylor, Paul Robinson, Hugh Young, T. Williams, Neville Mack, Stan Butcher, Glenn Johnston, Frank Nerney, P.R. Stephens, Tony Yelash, S. Cleland, S.S. and J. McGill and the dozens of talkback respondents to radio programmes in which I participated in most parts of the country.

This collection adds my continued collecting over the last few years, including some of the new computer slang. Some of it may soon be as dated as the verb 'to be lomu-ed' from Jonah Lomu's comet-like trail across the international rugby scene, which I have cut from this collection. I am already pondering the staying power of such new entries as my daughter and her sub-teen friends using 'scody' to indicate approval or disapproval, and the sudden emergence of 'tukus'. That is the nature of slang, language developing at the street and school and social level, much of it disappearing before it ever makes the formal records. If the slang from previous collections has already died out of use without ever making much of a mark, I have discarded it.

I have avoided cross-references or any referral to another page of the dictionary, having always found such entries irritating, when it is as easy to put the reference where the reader is. With the intention of keeping the book accessible and obvious, I have reduced abbreviations to a minimum. The common ones are 'C' for century, as in 'C19th' for nineteenth century, 'c' for circa, which means about or approximately the date, as in 'c1920', and 'WW' for World War as in 'WWI' for World War One. I have only put examples in quotes when they are quotes from somebody, or direct speech that could confuse in the context if it lacked quote marks.

I make no apologies for this collection, some of which can be used offensively. However, slang is mostly and almost by definition used for fun, and sometimes to defuse tensions with mock abuse. That is probably why, for instance, I often collected Maori entries from Maori themselves. The offence is in the mind of the beholder who is not considering the context in which slang flourishes, everyday conversation among all us ordinary Kiwi jokers. A feminist reviewed an earlier Kiwi slang collection of mine with the express purpose of finding sexist fault, and did have herself a field day, even unto deciding I represented one of my entries, namely 'root-faced'. I blame the mischief-maker who asked her to review a book she would not be seen dead purchasing. Pity she did not consult other collections of slang from around the world, including Partridge, for in these she would find even more offence against her decontextualised sensibilities.

Slang among its many civilising qualities is the yeast that leavens the dough of official reports, and it is popular with and familiar to most of us. This I am sure is why politicians like to use slang, to show the voters they are one of them, and to ease the pain of the stifling prose that bureaucratic and judicial minds employ to solemnise and mystify their proceedings. If politicians do not communicate, they are not good at what they do. Slang is a sure bet for getting across their message. Slang is the opposite pole from obfuscation, being the language we use when we are relaxed. It is our wordplay. This is where we can all be poets, for slang is metaphor. Slang tells us what we are like with our guard down. It defines us as Kiwis, warts and all. Before you write protesting to the publisher that much of it is in your view Australian or English, pause to consider whether maybe we used it first, or at least about the same time, or perhaps use it with slightly different emphasis and make it our own. We are such travellers, we export as well as import words and phrases. After all, our vowel sound has recently been identified as being exported. Why not the words too? In this informal area, nobody can claim absolute authority. In slang we are all qualified users. As our cookery experts say, enjoy.

5

A over K

a into g Arse into gear, usually intended to advise a hurry up.

a over k Arse over kite, a wild tumble.

AB A woman's monthly period, an abbreviation of 'Annie Brown'.

ab-fab Total approval, an abbreviation of 'absolutely fabulous', teen jargon from the 1950s.

ace Alone, as used in the phrase **on one's ace**.

acid Pressure; usually in the phrase **to put the acid on**, meaning to apply pressure. Probably derives from the acid test in chemistry to determine components.

acre Buttocks. Late 1930s.

across the ditch Australia, as being over the Tasman Sea.

Association of Consultants and Tax-dodgers A jokey nickname for the ACT political party.

act the goat/the giddy goat/act up Silly behaviour of a high-spirited nature.

Adelaide rugs Blankets made from used flour bags stitched together, first used by goldminers last century, named after bags' place of origin.

afghan A popular biscuit deriving its name from the cocoa colouring.

aftermatch function A boozy celebration after the game, usually restricted to males.

agatie A mottled marble resembling an agate.

alchie Alcoholic, often the outdoor variety.

all aboard! Call to start shearing, derived from nautical and coaching cry, now obsolete.

allakufic A quicker, cuter way of saying 'couldn't give a fuck', in the sense of not caring.

all around the pig's arse there is pork Reinforcement of the obvious, a phrase which is often resigned in delivery, sometimes tinged with sarcasm, akin to 'Is the Pope a Catholic?'

All Blacks The New Zealand national rugby union team, from the colour of the strip and mythologically maybe from a printer's error of an extra 'l' in 'all backs'. Prime Minister Seddon arranged for the *Daily Mail* to cover the 1905 British tour and reporter Buttery wrote of 11 October match against Hartlepool clubs, won 63-0 by New Zealand, that the whole team played with precision and speed as if they were 'all backs'. The typographical error was repeated in reports of two subsequent games. When the team arrived at Taunton to play Somerset, they were welcomed by 'All Backs' posters. *Punch* magazine confirmed the matter by asking Seddon in November: 'Can it be your head is turned by your team of Rugby "Blacks"?'

all cock and ribs like a musterer's dog Very thin animal or human.

allegation has been made and I intend to find the alligator, an Remark attributed in recent times to Tom Skinner, longterm postwar president of the Federation of Labour, but in the 1880s Dick Seddon used the phrase in a debate in the House of Representatives.

alley A two-up school. The phrase **to make your alley good**, meaning to better your prospects or status with someone, is probably from the other meaning of an alley as a marble, an abbreviation of alabaster.

all hair oil and no socks Flashy but unimpressive; often used of a superficially impressive performer, who ultimately disappoints.

all hands and the cook A situation involving everybody present, a nautical phrase moving mid-C19th on to the land, where 'hands' became farm workers.

all hands to dance and skylark Encouragement to have a rousing good time.

all hunched up like a dog on a bag of staples Looking extremely uncomfortable.

all over the place like a madwoman's shit An unacceptable situation, often used scornfully of a sportsperson who falls below expectations.

alpha geek The most knowledgeable person in the office.

aluminium rain Debris from a mid-air collision.

amber fluid Beer.

am-dram Amateur dramatic, usually dismissive of a production or performer judged to be below professional standard.

angel gear Coasting your car downhill with the ignition switched off. 'Engine off, no brakes, just a straight, silent run', the *Dominion* newspaper review 30 September 1989 of *Angel Gear*,

Colin Hogg writing on Sam Hunt as travelling poet performer. In England the phrase used to mean women's clothes.

angry man, the New Zealand soldiers used this term to describe the enemy in North Africa in WWII.

anklebiter An infant crawling around at about the height of a small dog and humorously supposed to display the same tendency to nip at ankles.

any sodium glutamate of yours is a sodium glutamate of mine Another way of saying 'any friend of yours is a friend of mine'; used among young people not unacquainted with the favoured seasoning in some Chinese takeaways.

Anzac Acronym for the Australian and New Zealand Army Corps from WWI.

Aotea biscuit Brown sugar, cornflour and cornflakes biscuits.

Anzac biscuit Firm, teeth-challenging coconut biscuit.

Anzac button A safety pin or a nail.

Anzac hare Meat loaf.

Anzac shandy Champagne and beer.

Anzac wafer A hard army biscuit.

apple 1. $100 bill, arrived at in a roundabout way from the rhyming slang 'apples and spice' for 'nice'.
2. Guts or intestinal fortitude, usually directed at a contact sportsperson

falling below the aggressive par expected.

apples Desirable state, usually in the phrase offering reassurance, **she'll be apples**, same derivation as above.

are your arms and legs painted on? A sarcastic way of suggesting you do something yourself.

arse into gear, get your Advice to somebody proving sluggish.

arse like a working bullock Big buttocks; the phrase can be approving or disapproving.

arse over kite Head over heels. Raconteur Brian Bell described a haymaker punch from poet James K. Baxter, concluding 'arse over kite I went into the gutter'. They were fighting over a woman after a 21st birthday party in Wellington in 1954, Bell relating the story in the 1972 Baxter memorial volume.

arse over tit As above, used from 1910.

arsepaper Despicable or useless person or thing.

Arse-ups The Fourth Battalion of the New Zealand Rifle Brigade in WWI, from their shoulder flash. AKA **Dinkums**.

arsey-boo A mess.

arsy-tarsy A tangle.

Arthur or Martha A confused male, usually described as not knowing if he's Arthur or Martha, from the era before men publicly declared themselves to be women.

Arty Farty Ngati Karate Club A pretentious group; also known as wankers.

arvo Afternoon, in its diminutive form.

as The conjunction minus the expected comparative clause, used to maximise or increase the impact of a statement; as in **I was hungry as.**

as big as the Waimak Big-hearted; from the large Christchurch river the Waimakariri.

as black as the inside of a Solomon Islander Very black and very dated.

as cold as a stepmother's breath Very cold. The stepmother may have replaced the mother-in-law as the traditional family *béte noire*.

as flat as a strap A flat plain.

as low as whale shit About as unacceptable as a person can be.

ask the question/ask the big question Whether a challenge can be responded to, the answer implied. An example was: 'And now the big question is being asked of Waikato,' from John McBeth commentating on TV1 on the game between Waikato and New Zealand Maoris, 8 July 1995, at the stage when the Maoris were drawing away and Waikato needed a huge effort.

ate the cow and worried the tail Leftovers.

Auckland cove Nickname for Aucklanders last century.

Aussie Diminutive of an Australian.

Australian haka, the A transparent attempt to avoid paying your way, developed in a television ad in which a group of drinkers inform one it is his turn to shout. He pats pockets vigorously and then whines, 'Where's me flamin' wallet?'

away laughing Some task that is or is likely to be readily achieved, as in the sentence: 'The America's Cup guys are away laughing.' The English have a longer phrase 'away you go – laughing'.

away with the fairies/pixies Not paying attention, sometimes because a person is mentally deficient, usually because they are not focused, maybe daydreaming of something unrealistic, such as a favourable response to a request for a date from Petra Bagust or Lucy Lawless.

B

Bagful of busted arseholes

bach From about 1900 a humble weekend or holiday hut or cottage by sea or lake or wilderness, cobbled together from secondhand or free odds and ends, raddled furniture, cold showers, outback toilet. In recent times also a more salubrious residence that can become a retirement home. Last century a bach was stand-alone spartan rental accommodation only big enough for the many bachelors who developed this country.

bachelorise Male making do when his female partner is away, or males flatting together.

bacher Occupant of a bach or a type who prefers to live alone.

baching Looking after yourself, often a male living alone in a hut or crude accommodation.

back of beyond Really remote place.

backblocker Dweller in remote rural area, perceived as crudely civilised.

backblocks Remote place.

backbone of the country Farmers, whose primary produce is the country's main earner.

baffle with bullshit Deceive.

bag To disparage or knock someone, such that they have received a **bagging**.

bagful of busted arseholes Ugly person or unpleasant condition, such as a hangover, usually preceded by some comparative phrase such as 'He looks like a ...' or 'I feel like a ...'

bail up To confront or constrain; a diminished version of the C19th bushranger's command.

banana Disparaging term for New Zealand-born Chinese, suggesting yellow on the outside, white within, used by immigrants about local Chinese.

bandicooting Artfully and craftily removing root vegetables not your own. A term imported here from Australia in the 1930s Depression, named after the marsupial that occasionally disturbs Aussie gardens.

bang An all-encompassing intensive, often used in the phrase **the whole bang lot**.

bang on 1. Precisely right or accurate, often used approvingly, as in 'that homebrew was bang on'.
2. To hassle, as in a pupil complaining that teachers 'bang on you'.

bang, go with a Successful activity, something often said of a party.

banged up Pregnant.

bangs like a leaky pipe when the tap's turned on/like a shithouse rat/like a dunny door in a high wind etc. Sexually enthusiastic partner.

banjo 1. Head-high tackle, probably imported from Australia. 'The old banjo,' said commentator Keith Quinn on TV1, 25 August 1990.
2. Leg of mutton, from its supposed similarity to the popular Australian name for a frying pan or shovel.

bantie Bantam fowl.

Barber, the The wind scything off the Mawhera River into Greymouth.

barbie The barbecue.

bark To vomit.

barker's egg Dog dropping.

barker's nest A pile of dog droppings.

Barn Dance, the The diagonally-striped pedestrian crossing in action, named after its inventor, New York City Traffic Commissioner Barnes; in

use since about 1950.

barrack 1. Cheering for a team, originating from the Northern Irish term for bragging.
2. Jeering, from its Scottish use.

barracouta Long, narrow, crusty loaf reminiscent of the fish of that name.

barrelarse Short and stubby person.

base bludger/walloper/wallower Dismissive term for military bureaucrat and/or officer, a Kiwi soldiers' extension of the 'base wallah'.

bash 1. A party.
2. To abuse verbally or physically.
3. Tramping term for difficult terrain.

bash, give something a Make an attempt, often an understated Kiwi statement of intent, as in 'That climb looks on, I'll give it a bash.'

bash artist Somebody too ready to use fists to solve frustrations.

basket case Somebody adjudged mentally deficient.

Basin, the The Basin Reserve oval sports ground in central Wellington that is a gem among international cricketing venues. Result of the 1855 earthquake lifting the land and draining a large pond.

bathers/bathing togs Swimming apparel.

battle Make pregnant or make love. Vince Boyle of Winton, researching the history of Mossburn, recorded a former wagoner in northern Southland in 1914 'battled a woman'. He had intended to marry her, until a few days before the wedding she had her teeth removed and sent him the bill.

battler Dogged worker or performer, often in sport, generally admired for honest endeavour, even if skill factor is modest. In the past has meant a swagman and also a prostitute working on her own without a pimp or brothel.

Bay, the The provinces of either the Bay of Plenty or Hawkes Bay.

beachcomber Shoreline scavenger, noted here by Edward Jerningham Wakefield in the early 1840s, before the *Oxford Dictionary* recorded the word.

beacher Retired whaler or sailor in the earliest Otago days.

beat about the bush Prevaricate.

beat to death with a stocking full of hot crap A jocular threat perhaps first heard in Bendigo, Central Otago.

beaudy/beaut/beautee/bewdy Appreciative exclamation, also used as appreciative adjective or noun, as in, respectively, 'That goal. Beaudy!'; 'That was a beaudy goal.'; 'That goal was a beaudy.' Often accompanied by a reinforcing word, as in 'wee beaut', 'little beaudy', 'you beauty' and 'you blimmin beaut'. In the phrase **to put across a beaudy**, you have been praised for a successful trick.

Beaver Station Blenheim in its flooding days of yore, attributed to Sir Joseph Ward or an unknown squatter.

beef bayonet/bugle Penis.

Beehive, the The nickname and indeed the only name for the cone-shaped concrete maze designed for the New Zealand Cabinet and staff by Sir Basil Spence, obviously named after its shape suggestive of a beehive, without any implication that drones or a queen bee are resident within.

been there, done that A dismissive remark indicating speaker knows all about something.

beer goitre Large, generally collapsed stomach from excessive beer drinking.

beer sandwich A liquid lunch.

beeswax! Rubbish! Rhyming slang with 'cracks', which are what cheeky people make. Usually used in the phrase **mind your beeswax**, meaning to watch your manners.

beggars-on-coals Damper or the unleavened bread made from flour and water and cooked on an open fire.

bell-topper Silk hat in New Zealand c1853, Australia c1859.

belly-buster A diver's stomach hitting the water.

belt A stiff drink. **To belt down** is to drink alcohol quickly; **to belt one on** is to get very drunk.

Bench, the The seat on which the rugby reserves sit awaiting the call on to the field.

bender A Catholic, from the bending of the knee to genuflect upon entering and leaving church.

Ben Doon and Phil McCavity Two mythical Celts inviting an easy laugh that glosses over uneasy feelings about homosexual activity.

benedict A recently married man, particularly if he was considered a confirmed bachelor. **Bachelors and benedicts** was a contest between married and single men.

berkers/berko Somebody considered excessively silly or angry, crazy or out of control, as in berserk, usually in the phrase 'to go berko'.

bet on two flies walking up the wall/across the ceiling Betting enthusiasm that knows no bounds, usually used of a compulsive gambler.

bet your balls Guarantee to and probably from a functioning male; eg Bet your balls that's the last time he shows his face around here.

better to bust your arse than die a cripple Encouragement to do some task to your utmost, rather than be left wondering and wimpish.

bible-basher A clergyman or layman given to excessive Biblical proselytising.

bickies/bikkies 1. Money, often in the phrases **big bickies**, for lots of money

or some operation that is on the grand scale and will usually involve big amounts of money, and **small bickies**, a paltry sum of money, often used dismissively.
2. Biscuits.

biddy-bid The Maori plant piripiri.

biffed Bothered; eg I couldn't be biffed doing that.

big ask, a Difficult achievement. Sports commentators refer this way to a player or team trying to overtake an opponent who is well ahead. In the second cricket test between New Zealand and Pakistan in 1994 New Zealand's task was described as 'a big ask'.

big girl's blouse Weak, timid wimp, often addressed disparagingly to an effeminate or irresolute man.

big-note To boast. From about 1935.

Big Smoke, the A large town, in the surrounding rural perception.

big spit, the To vomit.

Big Wet, the Continuous downpour for days, so-called by Aucklanders rightly fearful it will spoil sporting fixtures. One amply justified example was before the Bledisloe Cup test on 22 July 1995.

big wraps on, have Be highly impressed. The *Sunday Star-Times* for 23 June 1996 said Little 'has big wraps on Andrew Mehrtens' the incumbent All Black first five-eighths Little plays outside.

bigger than the back of an ARA bus
Very big, often in reference to the size of someone's bum; the letters stand for Auckland Regional Authority.

bigger they are, the harder they fall, the Instant proverb coined by Timaru blacksmith Bob Fitzsimmons, probably after he became world heavyweight boxing champion. He complained in 1902 that the force of his blows was breaking bones in his hands 'like pieces of chalk'. Bob and his phrase became a legend for defiance and fearlessness. *The Harder They Fall* was the title of the book and film of Budd Schulberg's exposé of bigtime boxing.

bikie Member of a motorbike gang.

Bill Masseys Army boots, after WWI Kiwi War Minister Bill Massey. Also known as 'Masseys', while the First Contingent of the NZEF were known as 'Bill Massey's Tourists'.

billy Tin can with a wire handle for boiling water over an open fire. Also a can with a lid for carrying milk. Both uses combine in making tea. Hence, **billy-tea**, which is made by tossing tea leaves into the boiling billy. The word has extended into the phrase **to boil the billy** meaning to make tea, and to stop for a tea or refreshment break, the latter meaning also in the phrase **to sling the billy**. A **billy boy** is the tea-maker, a **billy fire** is the outdoor fire for the purpose of boiling the billy, a **billy-can** is a billy, a **billy-hook** is the hook to hang the billy on, while **billybread/cake/loaf/ sponge** are all cooked in a billy, prob-

ably one with a lid. You can get sets of billies fitting one inside the other like Russian dolls, known as a 'nest', probably from Scottish word for a pot.

billycart Trolleys boys of all ages cobble together from bits of wood and spare wheels, probably less finished than the original carts pulled by billygoats.

binder A solid meal, from tramp slang about 1932, usually in the phrase 'to go a binder', meaning to eat a meal.

binocs Binoculars from c1945.

biodegradable Poms Kiwis, as described by Australians.

bird Easy, as in the phrase 'make a bird of'.

birdcage Used-car dealer's lot, from postwar era when chicken wire was still prominent. The dealer was known as a **birdcage boy**.

bite on, to put the To seek a loan.

bitser A mongrel or any other object that is made from disparate bits, such as a billycart.

bivvy Bivouac.

Black Budget, the The name was given to a deflationary 1930 budget taxing popular items, but now linked with the 1958 budget of non-drinking, non-smoking, non-conformist Minister of religion and Finance Arnold Nordmeyer, which taxed items such as beer and cigarettes.

blackbait Gutty bait or whitebait which have been in fresh water long enough to develop intestines. Scarcely edible, tasting a bit like sardines.

Black Magic The name of the successful Kiwi yacht in the contest for the 1995 America's Cup, having won all but one of the challenge races for the Louis Vuitton Cup and then whitewashed Stars and Stripes 5-0 to take the auld mug.

blackman Treacle, in the early C20th favourite, bread and blackman.

blacksmith A poor station cook who burns the food.

blades of meat Feet; rhyming slang.

Blenheimers Loss of memory from too much wine. A play on Alzheimer's disease and Blenheimer wine.

Blerta Acronym for Bruno Lawrence's Electric Revelation and Travelling Apparition. A group of musicians and entertainers travelling the country in the 70s, still with a cult following. Many went on to successful solo careers, such as singer Beaver, artist Fane Flaws, actors Ian Watkin and Tony Barry, film director Geoff Murphy. Bruno became the country's favourite actor, starring in such successful Kiwi films as *Goodbye Pork Pie* and *Smash Palace*. David Charles 'Bruno' Lawrence died of cancer on 10 June 1995 aged 53.

bless your garters Folksy phrase of gratitude.

blighty Blight bird, now known as waxeye, white-eye or silvereye.

blimey, Charlie! Expression of mild-mannered relief; watered down from its Cockney origin in 'Gorblimey', meaning 'God blind me'.

blimmin The mild version of 'bloody', sometimes in the phrase **blimmin eck**, where 'eck' is 'heck', a euphemism for 'hell'.

blinded with science Brains defeating brawn, in its derivation from the rise of the scientific boxers such as Gentleman Jim Corbett, at the expense of bruisers like John L. Sullivan. The phrase was extended during WWII to mean bewildering or overwhelming somebody with a mass of detail.

block A pack rape or female subjected by a group of men to serial sexual activities, often associated with bikie gangs in the phrase **to put/go on the block**.

block/bun/scone, do your Lose your temper, where the noun means 'head'.

block, use your Advice to show common sense.

blocked Satisfied, usually in regard to food.

blokery Mates who are men, particularly bachelors, earlier this century.

blood alley Whitish marble with red streaks through it.

blood's worth bottling Splendid fellow.

bloody oath! Affirmative intensive, as in response to the question whether you want your champagne glass topped up.

blow a tank Dynamite a safe open.

blow, have a 1. Sniff of glue, among streetkids.
2. A stroke of the sheep shears.

blowhard Boaster.

blowie A blowfly.

blow in Unexpected arrival.

blowing/blowing off Boasting.

blow me down with a fence post! I am surprised. Kiwi landed version of nautical 'blow me down'.

blow that for a joke! A phrase of rejection.

blow through Depart, perhaps in a hurry, or simply be passing through a place without stopping.

blow trout Use gelignite; a blow-back usage from catching fish by dynamiting their environs.

blow up 1. Referee use of whistle to stop play.
2. To confront somebody.

bludge To cadge whilst loafing, consuming without working like those around you. A bludger lives off others, a dole-bludger lives off State

benefits. Bludger's Hill was the name for the New Zealand Divisional Headquarters on a rise in the Maadi camp near Cairo during WWII, where the jobs were considered safe and occupants were perceived as shirking the frontline fighting. Derives from the prostitute's bully and his inclination to bludgeon problem clients.

blue 1. A brawl.
2. A mistake.
3. Red-haired person.
4. Drunk, perhaps from its association with blue devils that appear in extreme cases involving the drinking of methylated spirits.

blue-arsed fly, running around like a A dithery condition akin to a blowie after being hit by flyspray.

blue duck A failure or a lost cause, as in 'This super tax is a blue duck.'

blue fit/blue vinegar fit Extreme anger or shock or drunken behaviour, as can follow the imbibing of blue vinegar or turpentine.

blue lady Methylated spirits, which has a blue tinge.

Blue Orchid Member of the Royal New Zealand Air Force, whose blue uniform was considered namby-pamby by the khaki army lads.

blue rinse brigade/set Middle-aged ladies comfortably off, distinguished by the blue rinse through their well-tended hair, often wearing twin sets and pearls, to be found in National Party blue ribbon enclaves such as Remuera, Kelburn and Fendalton.

Blue Skin Whalers' name for Maori with tattoos.

blue veiner/blue vein flute The penis.

bluey 1. Half-gallon of beer. In England it used to be a measure of a half-pint and a pint, here it could relate to the anticipated effect of the blue devils from imbibing methylated spirits.
2. The bushman's blue blanket in which are rolled up his worldly possessions, such that **humping one's bluey** is only an innocent version of leaving home to travel, not some disgusting deviancy.
3. A summons to court, once a traffic ticket, from the colour of the paper, and a ban on entering a bar.

blunt as a bull's ear Very blunt; used by Otago high country farmers about poorly sharpened sheath knives.

blurter The anus, which blurts or emits noxious noise.

board Floor of a shearing shed, from which comes a **full board**, the shearing crew, and spin-off phrases: **to be on the board**, at work shearing; **all on the board!**, the cry marking the last sheep in the holding pens for the end of the shearing session; **off the board**, to be dismissed from shearing; **to walk the board**, to be controller of shearing.

boar's nest A mess. Rhyming slang; eg 'It was supposed to be selective logging, but it's a boar's nest.'

boatie Small boat operator.

bob each way, to have a Hedging your bet, probably from putting a bob or the imperial shilling on a win and a place in horseracing. Decimalisation in 1967 made shillings and pence obsolete, but words like 'bob' and 'penny' linger on in popular phrases.

bob-in A shilling contributed to the kitty or pool.

bobbycalf Milk-fed calf slaughtered very young for its tender flesh. Also known as a vealer. Defined by the Bobby Calf Marketing Regulations as a calf intended for human consumption as boneless veal. From the British dialect 'bob', a young calf.

bobsy-die A fuss. Often used in the phrase **kicking up bobsy-die**. From the British nautical rhyming slang 'bob's a dying' for 'idling', sometimes appearing in that form, as Ngaio Marsh in *Surfeit of Lampreys* writing 'It plays Bob's-a-dying with the whole blooming case.'

bodgie 1. Australasian male youth of the 1950s acting tough in copycat versions of rebel British and American gear such as greased-back hair, long, thin sideburns, black leather jackets, stovepipe trousers, white socks and winklepicker shoes. Originally American slang for a male jitterbug with long hair and oversized sports jacket.
2. Now means something of dodgy quality or origin, such as very cheap stereo equipment in sidestreet stores.

bogacka/bojack Pukeko. Pakeha corruptions of the Maori word for the swamp bird.

bogan Idiot or misfit. Pupils of St Patrick's College, Silverstream, suggested a bogan would be a long-haired, heavy metal listener.

bog in Work hard at something, often the eating of a meal.

boiled dog Affectation; eg 'Don't come the boiled dog with me, mate. I know you grew up in a railway house in Papakura.' From about 1910. Probably from a combination of 'boiled shirt' and 'putting on the dog'.

boiler A tough old chicken or other just acceptable animal fodder judged fit only for boiling.

boil up To become angry. In use in 1874.

boil-up Brew of tea, often outdoors, often in the phrase **to have a boil-up**.

bolter An outsider or racehorse on long odds that wins; sometimes applied to humans, usually in the footrace context.

bomb Ancient vehicle or other dilapidated piece of machinery.

bomb-up Wild party with much boozing.

Bombay bloomers Baggy sports shorts; originally WWII servicemen's shorts, made in Bombay.

Bombay Hills Dividing line between civilisation and the peasants; actual hills just beyond Pukekohe used in the phrases 'south of the Bombay Hills' and 'north of the Bombay Hills'. 'It is a truth universally acknowledged,' wrote Helen Paske in the *Listener* of 9 September 1978, 'that any New Zealander living south of the Bombay Hills is culturally deprived.'

bomb-squasher Big marble, a menace to small marbles.

bone people Pakeha wearing Maori pendants or other carved ornaments as gesture of solidarity with Maoritanga, in perhaps an oblique play on Keri Hulme's book *The Bone People*. Used contemptuously of such people.

boner Penis, usually erect.

bong To hit somebody, usually on the head. Perhaps a combination of the British public school 'bonk' and the Aboriginal word for 'dead'.

bonny new nothing with a thistle/throstle/whistle on the end, a Answer to a silly question, usually from a child; eg 'Please, Miss, what's that s'posed to be?'

bonza/bonzer 1. Pleasing or regarded well. Less commonly a 'bosker' or 'boshta'. Possibly imported with the goldrushes from California, diminutive of Spanish word 'bonanza'. 2. A large marble that was highly prized.

booai/booay/booeye/boohai A remote place. Refers to Puhoi, 50 kilometres north of Auckland, which was so isolated in its early days, its pioneering Bohemians almost died of starvation. This Pakeha corruption of puhoi, the Maori word for dull, slow or phlegmatic, is used in the phrase **up the boohai**, meaning to be lost or in trouble.

booboo A mistake. Usually you **make a booboo**. Extended from the American 'boob' with maybe a crybaby notion thrown in.

boob tat A tattoo acquired in prison, from 'boob', a prison.

Booka, Booka Maori colloquialism for the Bible c1815. By 1820 it was 'buka, buka', a book; by 1842 'pukapuka', meaning a book and the leaves of the rangiora shrub used as a substitute for paper at a time of paper shortage.

boomer First-rate, large, successful. Surfies talk of a boomer wave. A boomer is a large male kangaroo. Contrarily the phrase **a little boomer** can mean the opposite.

boonga/bunga Pacific Islander; an offensive adaptation of 'boong', an Australian Aboriginal.

boot, put in the/put the boot in Rugby union forward habit meaning to kick and stomp at any part of an opponent's body that comes between the booter and the ball. Also means any rough or unfair treatment of a vulnerable opponent.

boots and all Total commitment. Used as the title of All Black lock Andy Haden's autobiography. The All Black fullback Don Clarke was known as 'The Boot' because of his prowess at kicking goals and for touch. Used generally for any enthusiastic engagement.

boot home Strain to finish, from the racing term for urging the horse to cross the line first.

boot, in your Contemptuous expression akin to 'in your face'.

boots! Warning that the shearing boss is on the way.

boots leak, someone's That person is daft; eg 'Notice the way the new student stares into space? I'd say his boots leak.'

booze artist Drunkard.

booze barn Large tavern with ready access for consumption of alcohol.

booze rooster Drunkard.

boozer Hotel or tavern, or the person drinking to excess within.

boozeroo Drinking spree or place where you do it.

bo-peep A look.

borax Banter. Originally 'borak', almost invariably in the phrase **poke the borax at**, to tease somebody. From an Aboriginal word.

born in a tent? Sarcastic enquiry of anybody leaving a door open and letting in a draught, intended to make the offender close the door.

bot A bug or germ such as a cold or the flu, perhaps from the botfly whose larvae afflict farm animals. In the 1920s the bot signified a tubercular patient. **To have the bot** is to be in the grip of a cold or flu, or perhaps just feeling out of sorts and/or irritable. **How are the bots biting?** is a cheery greeting. **On the bot** is to be bludging or looking for a hand-out. **The bot** is a juvenile reference to junior's bum, or a jovial semi-euphemism, such as enquiring of somebody with piles, **How's the old bot?**

bottle drive A bottle collection to raise funds.

bottle-o A green marble, possibly recovered from the neck of a soft-drink bottle early this century, when the word also meant a dealer in empties and, by extension, a deadbeat or person of little account.

bottler A person or object of splendid account, often used in the phrase, 'you bloody bottler, mate'.

bottle store The room in the pub selling bottles of beer, wine and spirituous liquors.

bottlie The round glass stopper that used to be in the neck of softdrink bottles, recovered for playing marbles.

bounce the ball Testing public opinion, usually by politicians. From about 1920, from the habit of rugby union players, especially the first five-eighth, bouncing the ball to test the bounce before dropkicking off. The phrase evolved in recent times into **bouncing it off**, something favoured by advertisers in particular.

bowl To fell a tree or a deer or a pig, or to seduce a woman; eg for all four,

'Reckon I bowled her, eh?'

bowldacks Bullshit. Teenage Kiwi slang.

bowser 1. Petrol pumps from the 1930s, when the only ones available were made by Mr Bowser.
2. A dog.

box 1. Female genitals.
2. Mixing accidentally or deliberately two herds or flocks.
3. Muddling or making a mistake.
4. That dodgy area in rugby union games behind the scrum and in front of the last lines of defence, the winger and fullback: a clever opponent will **kick into the box**.

box and dice, the whole Everything.

box seat The most favourable place to be. Originally the position atop the coach taken by the driver, most famously Ned 'Cabbage Tree' Devine, the Central Otago goldrush driver who could turn his horses on a coin. Everybody wanted to ride in his box seat. He once refused the request from the Minister of Mines, saying it was taken. The minister informed Ned who he was. Ned replied that was a fine post and he should see he hung on to it.

boxed/boxed up Lost or bluffed, from the tramping term for getting lost.

box of birds Fit and/or well and/or deliriously happy. From WWII. Sometimes with the additions **and all singing** or **all feathers and shit**. Sometimes spelled **boxa birds**.

box of fluffies/box of fluffy ducks Fit, well and happy.

box on/box on regardless/box on with Persevere, originally in fighting.

box, one out of the Special person or thing. From about 1930.

box, to be in a To be in a confused state.

boxed-up 1. Imprisoned.
2. Confused.

boy 1. Polynesian man, used until recent times in sport, last century for a servant and/or missionary convert.
2. A greeting, particularly among Maori, as in 'G'day, boy, how's it goin.'

boya A man on the West Coast.

Boys on the Hill, the Members of Parliament, a hangover from when they were all male.

brain like a cow's udder Dim-witted. Brains or the lack of feature in a variety of scornful phrases, such as if **he had another brain it would be lonely** and **he hasn't enough brains to give himself a headache.**

brass razoo A minute, virtually worthless, imaginary coin, once approximating the status of a far-thing, usually used in the phrase **doesn't have a brass razoo.** Said to have been a gambling chip and/or to be a corruption of the Maori word 'raho', a testicle. Thus 'razoos' used for testicles.

bread and scrape/bread and spit Very little to eat.

breakfast, have for Boast that some-body or something will be easily con-quered or acquired.

break in Clear and cultivate new ground.

break it down! Take it easy, stop that, desist from speech. A command that is also usually a reprimand.

break out 1. A new goldrush last cen-tury.
2. A boozing spree this century, sometimes to the extent of vandalism.
3. The first cuts in shearing.
4. Hauling logs out of the bush.

brekkie Breakfast.

brewer's goitre A beer gut.

bride's nightie, off like a Hasty depar-ture. The variation 'up and down like a bride's nightie' indicates wild fluc-tuations.

bridge A glance.

Brit Person from Britain.

Britain of the South Early nickname for New Zealand, before Britain lost interest in us.

Britland Jokey name for Britain.

Briton Brave person, invoked as a role model for children, often in the phrase **Be a brave little Briton.**

bro Greeting, particularly popular

among Maori, short for 'brother'.

broken-arse A prisoner who has caved in to the system and goes to the bottom of the pecking order among his fellow prisoners.

broken-down swell An upper-class settler who has come down in the world, usually because of drink.

broomie Shearing floor sweeper.

bronzed Anzac Suntanned Antipodean.

brown Sulkiness and/or shame, in the phrase **do a brown**. Teenage slang.

brown derby South Island chocolate dip ice-cream.

brown-eye, to An unattractively active verb meaning to expose the anus.

brownie Cocoa or currant damper; treacle gingerbread among tramps.

brownie gorger A shearer.

Brown's cows In the phrase **all over the road like Brown's cows**, a disorderly state.

Browntable Establishment Maori. A play on the Business Roundtable group of business leaders. The *Dominion*, 5 August 1996, refers to 'Mr Henare ... contemptuous of the "Browntable" as well as the Pakeha establishment.'

brumbie/brumby Kaimanawa wild horse, probably from the Aboriginal word for wild, 'booramby'.

brush A woman, often as object of male sexual desire, the whole perceived from the pubic hair part.

buck/buck at To object. From c1890. In the phrases 'have a buck at' and 'to give it a buck' meaning to try something, maybe daunting. **Fair buck**! is an appeal to play fair, or an expression of astonishment.

bucket Harsh if not brutal criticism. Politicians give and take a bucketing.

bucket of pipis, goes off in the sun like a Promiscuous woman, in the perception of an insensitive male.

buck in Help the common cause.

Buckley's/Buckley's chance No chance. From convict William Buckley, who escaped and lived for 32 years among Aborigines before giving himself up.

buck Maori Well-built rural Maori. Used before WWII, and not much since.

buck rat, fit as a/wild as a Very fit or very wild.

buckshee leave Unofficial leave from the army, also known as going AWOL, or absent without leave. From the Arabic 'baksheesh', something for nothing.

buckshot Settlers' term for granulated lava in riverbeds, c1851.

budgie-cage Army detention centre or prison in WWII.

buffie Sultana, down south.

bugger it!/bugger me!/bugger me days!/bugger me sideways!/bugger that for a joke Expressions of surprise and anything else in context, such as disbelief or distaste.

bugger off! Expression of denial or dismissal, as in 'Bugger off! I never laid a finger on him.'

buggerama! Expression of mild or jokey distress.

buggerise about Aimless behaviour.

buggers afloat Doughnuts, dumplings or fried scones.

buggers-on-the-coals Currant damper.

build a feed Preparing food in the bush, originally South Island forestry workers and musterers.

buku Lots of anything. Army slang from Vietnam, mashing the French legacy of 'beaucoup'.

bull artist/bullshit artist Boaster or conman or experienced liar.

bulldogging Catching wild deer by dropping on them from helicopters. In his thriller *The Idiot Played Rachmaninov*, Michael Brown says it was so common in Westland that it no longer raised eyebrows there. Deer farming has made it almost obsolete.

bulldust Nonsense.

bullocky Bullock driver. To bullock is to act belligerently, while **bullocking**

over is a favourite description of how rugby union forwards crash in for tries.

bullocky's joy Treacle or golden syrup.

bull's foot, doesn't know B from a Ignoramus.

bullswool Nonsense.

bull the tea Put soda in your bush tea to boost its impact.

bullers Gumboots, from a brandname for a low-top, lace-up variety popular in bush country, usually cut down to lighten them, the laces replaced with wire and holes made in them to drain water.

bullet A cannabis cigarette, from its shape, invariably crimped at both ends to stop the crumbled leaf falling out.

bull-a-bull/bulli-bull/bullybul The flowering shrub poroporo, c1845.

bull's roar Not even close, in regard to the desired distance or objective; eg 'Norty's not within a bull's roar of qualifying for the sprints.'

Bullshit Castle Air Force headquarters, in the perception of our WWII airmen.

bully 1. A tiny freshwater fish, also known as a cockabully.
2. A bulldozer.
3. A pig-dog that appears to have a bulldog among its antecedents.

bulsh Nonsense.

bum bandit Active male homosexual.

bum buzzard A soldier sitting well back from the WWII action.

bumchum 1. Male homosexual.
2. Close friend.

bum man Male professing attraction for female buttocks, often in comparison with a professed preference for female breasts.

bum nuts Eggs, usually hen's eggs.

bumsquat The soldier safe back at headquarters or base camp in WWII.

bun A bowler hat, from its shape.

bun, do your Lose your temper.

bun-worry Fooling around, having a jolly time, from late last century.

bung 1. Ruined or bankrupted, often said to have 'gone bung'. From the Aboriginal word for dead.
2. Move something, as in 'Bung the plate over to me, will you.'

bung it on To boast or exaggerate.

bunga/bunger/bungy Early Pakeha versions of the ponga or tree fern.

bungy The elastic cord that once simply held items on your bike or car roof has been stretched around the ankles to allow **bungy-jumping** off disused bridges and other high places, often down to a ducking in the river below, before springing back up again.

bunking Skipping school.

buntuck WWI word for a rifle, our version of 'bundook', which had earlier meant a musket, and before that a crossbow. From the Arabic 'Banadik' for Venice, where crossbows were made. Venice is still Bundookia to Egyptians.

burgoo Oatmeal porridge among the WWI soldiers, possibly rhyming with stew, maybe with a reference to the enemy Turks' 'burghul', wheat porridge.

burk To dodge working.

burl Give something a try, such as a relationship or a restaurant.

burn Fast and probably showy driving of a vehicle, usually in the phrase **to go for a burn**, the burn referring to the smell of burning rubber when subjected to a fast take-off.

burn off Leave someone behind, usually by a rapid departure.

burn-off Clearing land by fire.

burst Drinking spree, usually in the phrases **on the burst** and **to have a burst**.

burst, on the Rugby union players advancing successfully through the opposition.

bush Forest or dense scrub. When you go bush you are leaving the city stress for the simple rural life, or you are hiding out.

bush baptist Religious ranter lacking the dog collar or authority of an organised religion.

bush carpenter A rough and probably untrained carpenter.

bush happy Somewhat deranged or eccentric person, from living alone too long in the bush.

bush justice The rough kind of justice decided without a properly constituted court.

bush lawyer 1. Laying down of the law by a layman.
2. A thorny native plant of the blackberry family whose clutches are not easy to escape.

bushman's breakfast A yawn, a piss, a look around.

bush mechanic Amateur and untrained mechanic.

bushranger Armed robber in the gol-drush days.

bush telegraph The grapevine or gossipy means by which information and rumour is spread.

bush whisky Illegally distilled whisky, almost invariably done out in the bush, such as the celebrated McCrae efforts in the Hokonui Hills of Southland.

bushed 1. Very tired.
2. Very lost.

bushie Bushman, a person who lives in and off the bush, like a forester or hunter.

bushwhacked Totally tired.

bust! Exclamation, usually of disgust. Often **Bust it!**, as my grandmother used to say when she dropped her crochet stitch and did not want to say anything stronger such as 'Bugger it!'

bust your boiler Collapse from over-exertion; eg 'Don't bust your boiler digging that crib wall.'

busy as a bee with a bumful of honey Very busy.

busy as a one-armed paperhanger Decidedly busy.

BUTA Boot up the arse.

butcher's 1. To be angry, usually **to go butcher's at**, from rhyming 'butcher's hook' with 'crook', in the sense of 'going crook' meaning to be angry with somebody.
2. A look, often **take a butcher's at.**

buttendski The buttocks.

buttinski To interrupt or butt in, from WWI soldiers.

buttonhole Sheep decrutching, with reference to the slang word for the genital area.

butterfly A rain cape or a coin that does not spin in the game of two-up.

buzz around like a bee in a bottle Busy and/or confused.

by Christchurch — hooya? Euphemism for 'By Christ, who are you?'

By korry/py korry Allegedly Maori pidgin for 'By God', elaborately presented in the nonsense rhyme:
'By korry said Hori to Hiki
We'd better sell our cows pretty slicky
For I've heard a mutter
That New Zealand butter
Comes from Bulls and Rangitikei.'

BYO Bring Your Own, wine usually, to a restaurant not fully licensed.

by the limping cricket/thundering sardine Mock horror oaths.

C

Cabbaging

Cabbage Train, the The Picton/Christchurch night train of yore.

cabbage-tree Hat made from cabbage tree leaves.

cabbaging Smoking cannabis leaves.

cabsav A cabernet sauvignon style of wine, a favourite Down Under.

cackleberry A hen's egg.

cactus In difficulty, in the phrase **in the cactus.**

call the game in Quit; eg 'Time to call the game in, fellas, the fish ain't biting.'

can-a-piss Beer in a can, the favourite drug of those who want you to know they do not smoke cannabis.

Cannabis County Northland.

cannon Rifle.

can't make honey out of dog shit You can't make something good out of something bad, like a silk purse out of a sow's ear.

Canterbury Pilgrim/Pilgrim One of the planned British immigrants to Canterbury.

Capital of Cow Country Hamilton.

Captain Cooker/cooker Wild pig, supposed descendant of those released in New Zealand by Captain Cook.

cardie Cardigan.

cark To die, if a person, to collapse if machinery, such as a car. To **cark it** is to die, but to **cark out** is to fall into a drunken sleep.

Carlaw Coathanger Stiff-arm tackle not unknown at Carlaw Park, the home of Auckland rugby league before the Auckland Warriors moved into Mt Smart Stadium in 1995.

carn! Come on! Often invoked by sporting spectators desperate for their team to do better.

carnie Sexually available female

under the lawful age for sexual intercourse; short for 'carnal' in the legal phrase 'carnal knowledge'.

carry matilda To carry one's swag or 'matilda'.

Cathedral City Christchurch, because of its central Anglican cathedral.

catch-up play A team having to come from behind to win a game; eg 'The All Blacks have to play catch-up football in the second half if they are to win the Bledisloe Cup.'

cats' bar The ladies' or lounge or private bar in the days up to the late 1960s when women were not permitted in public bars and had a private bar they could go with escort to be served liquor. From 'cat' meaning prostitute.

cattledog Catholic schoolchild, in the jeering language of State schoolchildren with rhymes such as 'Cattledogs, cattledogs, stink like frogs and live under logs.'

caught short Unexpected need to use the toilet, or menstruate without tampons available, or lacking means to host surprise guests or unable to meet a requirement for money.

cave in To defecate.

ceefa A cat, as in 'c' for cat.

Central Central Otago, radiating around Roxburgh.

chardonnay socialist A tepid socialist; used by Mike Moore in November

1993 of those Labour politicians planning his demise as leader of the party.

charge an arm and a leg/like a wounded bull Excessive pricing.

Charles Ulysses Farley Jokey variation of the dismissive remark 'Fuck you, charlie.'

charlie/charlie over the water A children's game like chasey or tag.

chateau cardboard Cheery term for cheap bulk wine in cardboard box.

chateau collapsio Cheap bulk wine in a weak cardboard box.

chati/chatty Louse to WWI Kiwi soldiers, possibly from Maori 'kutu', a louse.

Che Crown Health Enterprise, 90s name for a hospital now the government expects such places to pay their way.

cheeri! Short for 'cheerio' or goodbye.

cheerio Small saveloy usually served at children's parties with a large bowl of tomato sauce.

chelsea Sugar, from the name of the Auckland sugar works.

cherchez le sausage Sexual intercourse, a franglais play on the phrases 'cherchez la femme' and 'hide the sausage'.

chew To talk. From c1920.

chew/suck the kumara Something going wrong, often mechanical. Originally a topdressing pilot crashing.

chews Lollies, originally chewing gum dispensed by American servicemen in WWII.

chiack Vigorous teasing; also used as a verb. From the London street greeting.

chill out Relax, calm down; popular among teenagers.

chillybin Insulated plastic container for carrying food and drink.

Chinaman 1. Yellowish Central Otago stone that could have gold in it.
2. A chute for loading spoil onto trucks.
3. A length of wool on the sheep's rump the shearer left, looking like a pigtail.

Chinese burn Twisting wrist or leg skin between two hands, a children's playground pastime.

Chinese lady South Island toilet with many seats, indicative of low regard held for Chinese miners last century.

Chink A Chinese man.

chip To be impertinent; eg 'That boy chips me one more time, he cops it.'

chippie Potato chip.

chippy Wood-burning wetback stove; diminutive of chip heater.

chocolate trout A Taupo chocolate fish.

choice! Exclamation of enthusiastic approval.

choke a darkie To defecate.

choke it Stop something; eg 'Choke that radio, will ya.'

chook 1. Chicken, hen, even rooster.
2. Woman, often an older woman.
3. Silly person. Often said to be running around like a headless chook.

chookie Girlfriend or young woman.

chook's bum The mouth.

choom Englishman, to Anzac soldiers aping the Northern English pronunciation of 'chum'.

chop 1. Woodchopping contest, from late last century.
2. A fair share, often in the phrase in for one's chop. If something or someone is not much chop, it or he or she is of little value.

chop short of a barbie, a Mentally deficient.

chow Chinese.

Chowick Chinese resident in Auckland suburb of Howick.

Chrissie Christmas.

Christchurch!/By Christchurch! Euphemistic modification of 'Christ!'

chrome dome Bald person.

chuck/up-chuck To vomit.

chuck a mental/spaz/wobbly Lose temper or behave erratically. 'Spaz' is short for 'spastic'.

chuck it in Surrender or give up.

chuck off at To tease or abuse.

chuck-out Dismissal, usually the sack.

chuddy/chutty Chewing gum.

chuff Backside. Prime Minister Holyoake startled some people in 1967 when he talked about sitting on one's chuff, a phrase that usually means laziness.

chunder To vomit.

ciggie Cigarette.

City of Sails Auckland, which has more yachts to the nautical mile than anywhere else.

claddy Flax stem, a corruption of 'korari'. Glenn Johnston recalls as a kid at Kaihinu making the flax stalk rafts or mokihi, using them on the Houhou creek north of Hokitika.

clayie Clay marble.

Clayton's Anything phoney or imitation, from the advertisement for the non-alcoholic 'Clayton's — the drink you have when you're not having a drink.'

clean up Defeat, often used to indicate comprehensive sporting victory.

clever gear Fashionable or smart clothes, sometimes used derisively. 'What's with the clever gear, new date?'

client-server action Sex, in corporate speak.

clip around the ears with an iceblock, a Arrival of cold weather.

clog clatterer Dutch person.

clobbering machine The way the system allegedly squashes individuality, known as 'The Great Kiwi Clobbering Machine'. An Education Department report on Maori achievement in 1989 observed 'the great brown clobbering machine' of peer group pressure on Maori achievers in school and workplace.

clock To punch, usually in the head.

clocking Illegal winding back of vehicle odometer.

clucky 1. Gushing, often over a baby, in the way hens cluck contentedly.
2. Pregnant.
3. Showing fussy, gushy signs of wanting to be pregnant.

Coastie North Island East Coaster, mainly Ngati Porou and Whanau Apanui between Opotiki, the Cape and Gisborne.

coathanger 1. Close-pruned pine tree, the way it is supposed to be done.
2. Rigid arm across the neck, a very dangerous tackle in both rugby codes, whose practitioner should find himself in disciplinary trouble.

3. Auckland Harbour Bridge.

cobber A mate or friend, or sometimes merely the fellow alongside in manual labour. Cheery diminutives are 'cob' and 'me old cob'. The phrase **to cobber up with** is to make friends. From Yiddish 'chaber', a comrade.

cobbler The last sheep shorn, or a difficult sheep to shear. A pun on the cobbler's last. Recorded by Morris in *Straight Furrow*, 21 February 1968.

cockabully Grayling or small freshwater fish, a corruption of Maori 'kokopu'.

cocky A small farmer, like the cocky or cockatoo scratching out a small patch of earth. Often extended to calling a dairy farmer a **cow cocky**.

cocky's horror Grease and oil, which are never used by a dinkum cocky or farmer.

cocky's implement shed Any dumping corner for old farm machinery.

cocky's joy Treacle or golden syrup, which came in half-gallon tins in the days before fridges and was thus a thing of joy for several months, being the only food that lasted that long.

cocky's string Number eight fencing wire.

coconut Pacific Islander.

coconut bomber Nickname for the Third New Zealand Division serving in the Middle East in WWII, from their previous service in the Pacific and the implied doubt about its status as a war zone.

coconut tackle Head-high tackle. In March 1997 Northern Transvaal rugby coach Kitch Christie told the media: 'I first heard the term when I was in Dunedin a couple of years ago. I never considered the term racist. It is like referring to it as a mango tackle.'

cold as a frog's tit Very cold, or sexually frigid.

cold biting Begging in the Depression years in Australasia, when 'cold' meant cheek.

cold botting Begging for food door-to-door.

cold enough to freeze the nuts off a Massey Fergusson Very cold to anyone familiar with that brand of tractor.

cold pigging Selling goods door-to-door.

colonial Uncouth, provincial, naive, wet behind the ears. Still used by the British to put down New Zealanders.

colonial goose Mutton flaps stitched up in stuffing. Originally a boned and stuffed leg or shoulder of mutton, popular when these cuts were less expensive.

colonial oven Cast iron box with a door, placed in an open fire.

colonial pudding Basic steamed pudding made from flour, butter and whatever dried fruit to hand.

Colonial Robert Jokey name for a shilling, playing upon the proper name for a bob, or shilling.

coma'd Drunk to the point of being comatose.

come a thud A failure.

come at To attempt, often used negatively, as in 'Don't come at that with me, mate, or I'll drop ya.'

come good To succeed, something often said of sportspeople or racehorses after a period of disappointing performances.

come the uncooked crustacean Cause trouble, often by attempting to dupe. A variant on the popular Australian phrase 'come the raw prawn'. Often negative use, **don't come the uncooked crustacean**, meaning don't try to fool me.

come to light with To supply something, as in 'The coach finally came to light with the long-promised headgear.'

come up against To encounter difficulties.

Commo A Communist.

complexion like an oxidised potato An ugly face, perhaps pitted from boils or acne.

compo Financial compensation for work injury, or alleged work injury. The agreeable state of being **on** **compo** is to be receiving such compensation.

compo king Somebody perceived as illegally receiving compo from deliberately injuring him or herself, or pretending to be ill.

con-artist A deceiver, somebody practised at cheating.

Constantinople! A euphemistic and obsolete exclamation, converting 'Christ Almighty!' into the principal city of the WWI enemy, Turkey, now called Istanbul.

cooee Domestic hail, often calling the family to the dinner table, adapted from the Aboriginal 'guwi', a call. Something **within cooee** is available. If something is **not within cooee**, it is far from being attained.

cooker A wild pig, short for 'Captain Cooker'.

cooking with gas A fast solution. 'Sign this and we're cooking with gas.'

Cook's Tourists Second Echelon of the Second New Zealand Expeditionary Force, because they went to Britain in WWII.

cootie A head louse, from the Maori 'kutu'.

copper Maori A native oven, from 'kopa', a hangi.

coral stomper A Polynesian.

corker Anything appreciated, such as

people saying they had a corker time at a party. It may go back to the meaning of 'caulker', a dram of liquor.

corrie iron Corrugated iron sheets, for cladding roofs and sometimes walls.

cossie A swimming costume.

cot-case Somebody fit for the lunatic asylum, though it may only be a temporary craziness from too much alcohol.

could eat a horse and chase the driver Very hungry.

could eat an apple through a picket fence Buck-toothed.

could eat the crutch out of a low-flying duck Very hungry.

could open a can of peaches with that nose A prominent nose.

could play a piano while pouring concrete Can do anything, as Stu Wilson said of All Black centre Frank Bunce when playing for North Harbour against Auckland, TV1, 19 September 1992.

could scull the cap off a can of beer Very thirsty.

could you stop a Presbyterian? Would you like a shot of whisky in your tea? A Deep South of the Mainland question, cannily concealed.

couldn't bat an eyelid Adjudged an appalling batsman. This was the laconic opinion of cricket commentator Glenn Turner of Indian spinner Bhagwat Chandrasekhar, 3 February 1991. Chandrasekhar averaged about 4 in approximately 80 matches.

couldn't catch a cold if he/she sat naked all night in an icy pond Unlucky or incompetent.

couldn't fuck a frog trotting Inept.

couldn't hit a dead bull's bum with a tin can Without any discernible skill in the motor coordination department.

couldn't kick a hen off its nest Underachievement, a day to forget; eg 'Don Clarke had one of those days when he couldn't kick a hen off its nest.' T.P. McLean, *Evening Post*, 30 June 1995.

couldn't lie straight in bed A liar.

couldn't piss out of a boot with the directions written on the tongue Clumsy.

couldn't poke a sharp stick up a dead dog's arsehole Astonishingly incompetent.

couldn't see the road to the dunny if it had red flags on it Very drunk or very stupid.

couldn't sell a statue to a pigeon Ineffectual person.

couch potato Television addict.

country so poor a rabbit would have to take a cut lunch Poor farmland.

cow Problem person or thing, such as a cow of a motorcar.
cow-banger/cow-cocky/cow-spanker A dairy farmer.

cowsh Term of dismissal for something regarded as nonsense or rubbish, short for 'cowshit'.

cow's kipper Cow pat.

cow-tree Karaka shrub.

crack a fat To express a sexual erection.

crackee crackee Obsolete C19th Maori colloquialism for preaching. Maori borrowed the whaling word 'crack', to boast, and with it the whalers' attitude to missionaries.

cracker 1. Karaka tree.
2. Smallest amount of money, usually employed in the negative, as in **not a cracker** or **not having a cracker**.
3. Rated highly, as in a cracker day. Probably shortened form of 'cracker-jack'.
4. A cartridge. Usually plural.
5. The shredded end of the stockwhip or a flax whip, used in the phrase **Can he crack his whip?**, meaning 'Is he a good drinking man?' If somebody **cracks the whip**, they are urging or ordering greater effort or control, as a jockey cracks the whip over a horse's flank. In WWI the front line was known as 'where the whips are cracking' because the sound of battle was similar to whip-cracking.

crack on about Talk on and on past the listener's patience.

crappers ditch, in In trouble, as one would be if one found oneself in the place where people have crapped or defecated.

crash hot! Exclamation of strong approval. Often used in the negative, as complaining about **not feeling too crash hot** to indicate you are feeling lousy.

crawlie The koura or freshwater crayfish.

crayfish A contemptible person, as in one who crawls to authority blabbing about his mates. From the army in WWI.

cream To defeat comprehensively, often in competitive sports.

cream your jeans To ejaculate sperm, or to become excessively excited.

crib Holiday cottage in the South Island.

crib/cribtime Mealtime or smoko in the South Island.

cribtin Lunchbox, mostly on the West Coast of the South Island.

crim A criminal.

crimplene suit and Skoda brigade A group of Social Crediters, the suits often crimson.

crockery Teeth, as called by commentator Keith Quinn in the Ireland versus New Zealand second rugby test, 6 June 1992.

cronk Ill or dishonest, allied in the original use to make a racehorse sick to fix a race. From the German word 'krank', ill.

crook Ill or angry, deriving from 'cronk'. Often used in the phrase **to go crook**, meaning to display annoyance or anger. If you **feel** or **look crook**, you are ill or unhealthy. If you are **in crook with** someone, you are in their bad books. If someone **puts you crook**, they have misled you. If they **go crook on** you, your status has declined in their eyes. A **crook deal/job** is something that goes wrong, perhaps through bad luck, bad judgement or simply the fates conspiring against you. A **crook do** is a poor party. A **crook run** or **trot** is a period of bad luck. A **crook steer** is being given misleading information.

crookie Someone unreliable or plain bad and dishonest.

cross-eyed spieler A crafty character. The Yiddish 'spiel', the play, usually means to swindle.

Cross-roach A Kiwi bludger sponging in King's Cross, Sydney, a rough area of lowlifes and deadbeats and hookers and strip joints, where such activity would be regarded as at cockroach level.

crow A farmhand forker of hay or shoveller of grain.

Crowe-eaters Nickname for the New Zealand cricket team on its Australian tour of November 1989, a reference to two of its leading batsmen,

Martin and Jeff Crowe; in retrospect it may seem ambiguous, in that eating crow is an Americanism for being humiliated, whereas it was intended to mean that the Crowe brothers were going to be at the forefront of the Kiwi demolition of the Aussies. Jeff Crowe had already distinguished himself playing in South Australia, a resident of which state is known as a 'crow-eater'.

crown jewels, the The treasured male genitalia.

crumb-bum An oaf, by extension of the word crummy, meaning worthless.

crust Livelihood; eg 'It's no easier than it ever was to earn a decent crust.'

cucumber fish A by-product of whitebaiting that announces itself by its cucumber odour.

cuff, a bit on the To be unfair or severe.

cunning as a Maori dog Sly or cunning in a low fashion.

cunning as a shithouse rat Super sly or cunning.

cunning stunt Jocular greeting, the meaning bearing no relation to its origination in the swapping of letters between the two words 'stunning' and 'cunt'.

cunt's hair/red cunt's hair The measure of some minute mechanical difference.

cupful of cold sick, a Indicative of low esteem. A poor game of rugby might be so described.

curly Difficult or attractive. Depending on the context or which team you back, a cricketer could bowl a curly ball that was tricky or superb, or both. Often the addition of 'extra' indicates strong approval, such as 'That was an **extra curly** ball he bowled.' Cricket is probably where the word originated, where the ball can curl in mysterious ways.

Currie A bikie frequenting Currie's milkbar in Queen Street, Auckland, in the 1950s. The phrase might be hurled derisively at somebody acting hoonishly.

curry Aggressive encouragement, possibly abusive, not often physical anymore. If you give the team you are supporting a bit of curry, you are shouting at them to do better.

curry-muncher Term for an Indian or somebody intimate with an Indian woman.

cut A share, probably derived from sheep shearing, where to get a cut was to get a shearing job. When you are in for your cut, you anticipate a share. Furthermore, a cut could be

the completion of a job. If something is cut, it is finished or completed, such as a large keg of beer, or the person drinking it, who is drunk. If the drinker has not been excessive, he or she would be **half-cut**. If you take a cut, you accept a reduction in your share or salary. If you enjoin someone to cut out the rough stuff, you want them to calm down and/or stop being aggressive verbally or physically.

cut a track Leave, usually in a hurry; eg 'I've had this cannabis cultivation caper, I'll leave yous jokers to it and cut a track.'

cut cat, to go like a To exit smartly, as you would expect from a cat that had been cut.

cut the rough Desist from doing something aggressive or unpleasant to others, often used as an imperative against such rough stuff.

cut the cheese To fart.

cuts Corporal punishment. Usually termed the cuts, when getting the cuts involved pupil's hand being whacked by the teacher's cane or strap.

cuz/cuzzy/cuzzy bro Polynesian male greeting. Pakeha term for a Polynesian male.

Darth Vader's dunny

Daffodil Hill WWII base headquarters for officers, residing in a place perceived as yellow or cowardly by the frontline soldiers.

dag Entertaining, amusing or unusual person or thing. A funny person can be called **a real dag**. However, if you were to **rattle his dags** you would be shaking him up, urging him to get on with it. Allegedly from the noise of uncrutched sheep dags or excrement-coated hindquarters flapping together as a sheep moves.

daggish/daggy Definitely amusing, while 'daggy' can also mean wilting or dated clothes.

dairy Small neighbourhood general store selling everything from toothpicks and soft drinks to wrapped bread and sacks of coal from dawn to dusk seven days a week. Often run by new arrivals, nowadays especially Indians, who employ the whole family. Originally a shop for milk and still big on that and non-essential food items like sweeties and chippies, cigarettes, pet food, TV dinners and piles of newspapers and magazines.

daker A marble; variant of Australian 'dakes', marbles.

daks Trousers. Young male drinkers often enjoy 'dropping their daks' to expose themselves to each other and passersby.

Dallie A New Zealander whose ancestors came from Yugoslavia late last century, before it was called that, to dig gum up north. Mostly from Croatia, or the part of it then known as Dalmatia.

Dallie plonk Dismissive term mid-C20th for the rough, sweet wine produced by Dalmatian vintners for the sweet Kiwi palate, before Kiwis started drinking seriously the drier wine made by the same Dalmatians or their descendants.

damper Basic bush bread made from flour and water cooked in the ashes of an open fire.

dance a haka An expression of pleasure, from the Maori dance chant, from late last century.

dancing dolly The small storm petrel seabird that appears to dance over the ocean, wings flapping, legs trailing in the water.

dancing the Pommy waltz Dodging dog turds on the pavements of London.

dangle-parade Short-arm inspection for Kiwi soldiers in WWI.

Darth Vader's dunny The Bank of New Zealand headquarters in downtown Wellington, from its long black box appearance, supposedly suitable for the toilet purposes of the chief villain of the Star Wars films.

date The anus.

date driller Active male homosexual.

daylight robbery Excessive and unrepentant overcharging for goods or services, such as the entire system of the Goods and Sevices Tax to some free market libertarians.

dead as a moa Decidedly dead, as is the extinct, ostrich-like bird that once roamed New Zealand.

deadbeat Unlucky or broke individual.

dead house An hotel outhouse where gumdiggers expected to find drunks dumped.

deadman Anchor recycled to hold a pile of fence posts, specifically spars or poles in logging.

deadman's arm A leg of lamb.

dead right Absolutely correct; Steve Parr on *Sale of the Century*, 19 September 1989.

dead ring/ringer Close likeness. Possibly from 'ringer' meaning originally a horse that has been disguised to look like another.

dead tree edition/option Paper version of an electronic publication.

deal to Physically account for somebody. You can also **deal it out to**.

Debt Dodgers and Wife Beaters First Echelon, Second New Zealand Expeditionary Force, WWII, derisive assumption that is why they volunteered first to fight overseas.

deefa A dog, as in 'd' for dog.

Deep Thinkers Fifth Reinforcements of the Second New Zealand Expeditionary Force in WWII, with reference to them pondering deeply before signing up, the suggestion perhaps that they were in no hurry to fight for King and Country.

delec Delectable, in teen shortspeak.

deli A delicatessen.

delish/delishimo! Very tasty, short or long teen slang for 'delicious'.

demon A detective.

derision Filthy weather among trampers, as in 'shit and derision', an air force phrase for bad weather.

derro A derelict person, sleeping out,

usually the worse for booze.

des-res Desirable residence, originally real estate parlance.

devil Maori name last century for Pakeha settlers hostile to the missionaries, or for a Maori not converted to Christianity.

dew pond Natural or manmade waterhole, usually reliant on rain. Mainly lower South Island usage.

DH Down the hatch, or drink up; eg DH, lads, it's almost closing time.

Diamond Dinks Second Battalion, New Zealand Rifle Brigade, in WWI, from the shape of their shoulder flashes. The First Battalion were the Square Dinks, the Third the Triangle Dinks and the Fourth the Arse-ups.

diarrhoea bags Knickerbockers.

dick To lose; eg 'We got dicked by St Bernards 50-0.'

dicken/dickin/dickon Indicative of disgust or disbelief, usually in the phrase **Dicken on that!** Probably from 'dickens', a euphemism for 'devil'.

dickhead Idiot. The 'dick' is C19th military slang for penis.

dickwhacker Idiot, where 'whacker' is a masturbator.

dickydidoe Penis.

diddlydieday Reunion, on the West Coast.

diff Difference.

differ Difference; turn of the C20th usage.

dig/digger/old dig Friendly greeting, usually male to male. Specifically an Anzac soldier or returned Anzac serviceman. Originally a gold-digger, who worked 'the diggings'.

dig deep A supreme effort, as when the All Blacks had to 'dig deep' in the 1991 second test at Eden Park against the Wallabies for the Bledisloe Cup, having been walloped in the first test at Sydney.

digging for whoopcackers The answer to the question how come someone is so dirty?

digglers Eggs.

dilberries Goat excrement.

dill/dillbrain Stupid person. Origin could be from 'daffodilly', where 'daffy' meant silly, or the rhyming slang 'dillpot/twat', or 'dillpickle', a fool.

dindins Dinner.

ding A dent, usually in a car, or the accident that causes a dent, from the archaic verb 'to strike'.

dingbat Eccentric or crazy person. The plural means an extreme stage, as in delirium tremens from consuming excessive amounts of alcohol. The 'bat' extension probably prompted by 'bats in the belfry', a term for madness or eccentricity.

dinger Anything regarded highly. Short for 'humdinger'.

dingo Australian.

Dinkies A couple with double income, no kids.

dinkum Fair, genuine or reliable, from English dialect 'ding', to work hard, and **fair dinkum**, an equitable share. The validity of something is often attested to as 'fair dinkum' or **the dinkum truth**, whilst a New Zealander born and bred is a 'Dinkum Kiwi'.

Dinkums Fourth Battalion of the New Zealand Rifle Brigade. AKA **Arse-ups**.

dinky Small and neat or cute. We might distinguish between our big milk trucks and the dinky electric vans of the British.

dinkydi/dinkydidoe Absolutely okay, fair, true.

dinnyhayser First-rate. For those who still remember the Australian boxer Dinny Hayes.

dip one's lid Honour somebody in the old gentlemanly days, by lowering your head and raising your hat.

dip out Miss out on something, usually considered a failure, as so many every Saturday evening dip out on a Lotto strike.

dipper, in your Obsolete indignant challenge, probably replaced nowadays by 'Up yours!' Perhaps a reference to a sheep dip.

dipshit Idiot. Variant on 'dippy', meaning silly.

dip south Search your pocket for money, particularly when there is not much there.

directly Eventually. As in, 'I'll be there directly.'

Dirt-trackers Midweek non-test rugby players on tour.

dirty/dirty on Angry or upset. Rugby players are frequently described as being dirty on each other after a dirty tackle.

dirty big Very bloody big.

dirty play Illegal or unfair sporting intervention, such as the use of fists or boots in a rugby ruck.

disaster A small coin. Specifically an Egyptian piastre to WWI Anzacs. It signifies both rhyme and little value.

Ditch, the The Tasman Sea.

div The New Zealand Division among WWII soldiers.

divvy A dividend, usually a payout from the TAB.

do/do in/do one's dough To use up all your money, perhaps recklessly.

do a get To retreat in a hurry.

do one's block/bun/scone Lose your temper.

dob/dob in To inform on someone,

usually with the implication that this is not dinkum Kiwi behaviour.

dob over To drop-kick a ball over the rugby goalposts, which is literally closer than the previous entry to the English dialect word 'dob', meaning to throw down heavily.

doctor 1. A West Coast publican. The original was Dr Schroder of the Central Hotel, Fitzherbert Street, Hokitika.
2. A sheep-station cook; originally a ship's cook.

dog Large iron nail for securing rails to sleepers or wire rope to timber.

dogbox, in the In trouble or disgrace, from the word for railway carriages without corridors.

dog cock Chub-style sausage.

dog tucker Defeated. Speaker of the House Doug Kidd suggested in May 1997 that NZ First would be dog tucker at the next election.

dog's breakfast A mess.

dog's dinner Well-dressed, if you are **done up like a dog's dinner**. However, if you are **done like a dog's dinner**, you have been comprehensively defeated.

do-it-yourself Proud Kiwi home handyman tradition of repair and restoration of anything around house, garden, farm or bach.

dole bludger Somebody who prefers or is perceived as preferring Social Welfare benefits to working for a living.

Dolly Parton wine An up-front red.

dome Press stud.

domestic A family disagreement, so described by police called to the scene.

dommie A motorcyclist, after the diminutive for a Norton 'Dominator' motorbike.

dommyknocker A stick to beat other children with.

dong To strike or punch.

dong/donger/dunga/dunger
1. The penis.
2. An idiot.
3. A useless or dilapidated object, like a rusty old car.
4. If you are **in the dunga** you are in trouble.

dongyknocker A club, cousin of 'dommyknocker', invoking the concept of a dong or knock, such as a hunter might use to dispatch a possum.

donk A useless racehorse, one perceived as a donkey.

donkey A deer, to those who stalk them.

donkey deep Enthusiastic participation. Skipper Chapman of the Coromandel said on television, 12 April 1990, of fighting miners that if it was a boxing ring, 'I'd be in there donkey deep'.

don't be ankyfooken A dismissive rejection.

don't be an Uncle Willy Don't be silly (rhyming slang extension).

don't drink and drive home, smoke dope and fly home Flip advice from cannabis enthusiasts who assume dope is less harmful than booze.

don't eat peas through a tennis racquet An oblique way of saying you are ugly, and could make it worse.

don't get historical Goofy advice to calm down, spoonerising 'hysterical'.

don't get off your bike, we'll pick up the pump Advice to an angry person to calm down.

don't go in the roundhouse, Jenny A warning about going into a dark corner with a male, from the roundhouse or locomotive sandbox where lust might be practised unsussed. Maybe a reworking of the WWI song and catchphrase 'Don't go down the mine, Daddy'.

doodackie A thingummybob or object of uncertain definition but probably useful.

dook To duck, used in the phrase **dooking for apples**, ducking mouth underwater to recover apples using only your teeth. Recorded by Brian Sutton-Smith in his collection of children's games.

doolan An Irish Catholic, often a Micky Doolan, a popular Irish name.

dork 1. Stupid person.
2. The penis.

Dorkalofa Auckland.

dorkbrain Idiot.

Dorklander Aucklander.

DORKs Doddering Old Real Kiwis.

dosh Money, as in dollars and cash.

doub/dub/dubb Giving someone a lift on your bike, whereby the person sits on the handlebar or the carrier, as in doubling.

double-dipping Two incomes from the State, illegal for all but politicians and judges, who may do other work whilst keeping their pensions, called welfare fraud when sickness beneficiaries do it. Lawyer David Stevenson wrote about this practice in the *Evening Post* of 20 June 1991, paying particular attention to 13 retired judges the previous year earning an average of $54,000 each for relieving work whilst still drawing their pensions, which their British counterparts may not do. He singled out the Parliamentary Super-Brigade, each earning over $40,000 taxfree pension plus their directorships and consultancies and diplomatic plum jobs.

doughboy Suet dumpling favoured by musterers.

doughnut Round-patterned wheelies done in car or on motorbike.

down on, have a To hold a grudge or poor opinion of another.

down south 1. Somewhere in the South Island usually.
2. The trouser pocket bottom, where money may be unsuccessfully searched for.

down the coast diving for fish farts A deadend job.

down the road Dismissal from work.

down the rocky road to the funny farm Someone showing signs of mental instability, indicating the direction in which they are heading.

down to the wire Very close contest, only resolved at the finish.

down trou The lowering of trousers to shock or amuse, usually by inebriated males at parties.

Down Under New Zealand and/or Australia.

dozo Fool, somebody who is dozy in the brain department.

DPB Domestic Purposes Benefit, State stipend to impoverished family caregiver.

drack Ugly or boring, often directed at a plain female, without intending the extreme condition of the probable origin, the fang-toothed, blood-imbibing Count Dracula.

drag the chain Lagging behind in a group activity such as drinking beer in pubs. Originally slowest shearer.

drama queen Exaggerated performance to win attention; eg 'That kid's a drama queen, screams the place down whenever another kid bumps into her.'

dressed pie Pie in a brown paper bag with peas and potato and gravy on top.

drink the piss from a brewer's horse, would Devotee of booze.

drive the pigs home To snore.

driver is safer when the road is dry, The/And the road is safer when the driver is dry Don't drink and drive.

drongo Stupid or clumsy fellow. A poorly performed Australian racehorse of that name probably popularised the idea, though there is an Australian bird the 'drongo'.

drop 1. Get rid of somebody; eg 'Drop that boyfriend before he drops you.'
2. To knock someone down; eg 'One more word like that in front of the ladies and I'll drop ya.'
3. To give birth. Originally referring to farm animals.
4. To deliver sly grog.

drophead Idiot.

drop in it Put or leave someone in trouble, as in 'You dropped me in it with the cop saying it was my cannabis stash.'

drop off 1. To falter and fail. Racehorses and athletes 'drop off the pace' of a race, a rugby player 'drops off the tackle'.
2. To give someone a lift in a car to a particular place.

drop off the perch Die, as parrots and chooks do.

drop one's bundle 1. To lose your temper or composure or control of a situation.
2. To give birth to a baby.
3. To defecate.

drop one's gear Take off your clothes.

drop one's load A male ejaculation.

dropper Fence post.

droppie A drop kick at goal in rugby union.

drop shoulder Idiot.

drum 1. A horseracing tip, or any information.
2. A swag, rolled up in the shape of a drum for easier carrying.

drummer Swagman or tramp. In shearing slang, the learner in the shed, or 'drummer boy'.

dry area A neighbourhood that continues to vote against hotels or sales of liquor.

dry as a cocky's selection/a Pommy jockstrap/a sack of gum-dust/a wooden god Very thirsty, usually for a quantity of beer.

dry balls bastard Parsimonious bowler in cricket, who gives away few runs.

dry root Unlubricated sex.

dub in To contribute to a collection.

ducks and drakes 1. The shakes, from excessive drinking.
2. Somebody giving you a difficult or misleading time.

duck's arse A male hairstyle popular in the 1950s where haircream was used to shape the backsides together into a middle ruff reminiscent of a duck's bum.

duck away To avoid something or somebody.

duck's breakfast/dinner A drink of water among WWI soldiers.

duck disease Short or vertically challenged person.

duckshove To pass responsibility on to somebody else in an unfair if not cheating fashion. Bureaucrats are perceived as practised at what the Americans call passing the buck. From Melbourne cabbies last century jumping ranks.

duck's nuts, just the Very desirable, a variant of 'the bee's knees'.

ducks on the pond Warning among shearers that a woman is present.

duff To make pregnant, perhaps from resemblance to a suet pudding called a 'duff'.

duffer A failed goldmine.

dumb-bum Fool.

dummy 1. Person who acquires land on behalf of another, usually not entitled to do so. Nowadays the plant an auctioneer uses to bid up a house auction. 2. Prison cell, usually a punishment one, where being placed in dummy is to be in solitary confinement.

dump one's load Male ejaculation.

dungpuncher Active male homosexual.

dunny A toilet, from the British word 'dunneken'. The 'dunnaken-drag' was the cart that collected toilet refuse at night, the carter called the dunny man. His carrying the can on his shoulder gave rise to the phrase for someone depressed being **flatter than a shit carter's hat**.

dust Gunpowder, noted by E.J. Wakefield among whalers here before it was recorded elsewhere.

dustie Dust or garbage collector.

Dutch oven A camp oven, a round iron pot with a handle to suspend it over a fire and lift it off.

dry as a nun's nasty Alcoholically very thirsty.

dry horrors Antipodean extension of 'the horrors', the first stage of delirium tremens.

durry A cigarette, specifically a roll-your-own. The container for loose tobacco and cigarette papers was known as 'durries'. After the popular brand Bull Durham.

dyke A toilet, often the outdoor variety whose bottom is not in sight.

Easy as carrying a kerosene tin full of cow shit uphill on your head

earbash Talk aggressively at someone and/or incessantly. An **earbasher** is a person who talks too much.

early doors Early to bed.

early shower Banished from the field of play by the referee for a serious example of foul play.

earwag To gush gossip.

easies Woman's corset.

easy as carrying a kerosene tin full of cowshit uphill on your head Not easy.

easy as hooking an eel with a blunt pin Definitely not easy.

easy as shoving a pound of butter up a cow's bum with a size five knitting needle on a hot day Extremely diffi-cult.

easy come, easy go Resigned attitude to a lost gain, usually money; eg 'Doubled the value of me shares last year, this year they halved. Guess she's easy come, easy go.'

Eat more, root more, drink more piss Macho chant of the Red Squad formed to deal with anti-Springbok Tour protesters in 1981.

eat toot Period of adjustment to pio-neering life, when the new immigrant learns to cope with a harsh new life. From 'tutu', a posionous plant.

Ebony and Ivory Bernie Fraser and Stu Wilson, All Black wingers of the 80s and entertainers on and off the field, co-writing a book of that title at the end of their playing careers. They still entertain, mostly as commenta-tors on rugby.

educated boot Elegant, effective kick-ing for touch in rugby, usually by the first five-eighths, and at its more ele-gant off the left foot.

eggs are cooked, one's Visited by mis-fortune, if not disaster, as happens to farmers struck by floods or droughts.

eh? Unnecessary interrogative at the end of sentences indicating a national uncertainty or need for reassurance or agreement; eg 'We really put it to the Aussie cricketers, eh?'

el cheapo Inferior object, often used of a restaurant.

electric fireplace Television.

electric puha Cannabis.

elevator doesn't go to the top storey Somebody who is not too bright.

empty sack can't stand, An/A full sack can't bend Farming advice to labourers at harvest time to get on with the job.

emu parade Detention involving cleaning up the grounds.

enough to choke a bull A fat roll of money.

euchred Defeated or totally exhausted. From the card game 'euchre', where you win by frustrating the other players' ability to win tricks.

ever thought of renting your mouth out for a car park? Loud mouth.

every man and his dog Attracting a wide cross-section of society; eg 'Every man and his dog will love it.' 1990 television ad for a Holden ute.

everything but the cat's blanket A comprehensive effort; eg 'The New Zealand Fifteen hit the Romanians with everything but the cat's blanket.' Keith Quinn commentating on Kiwi power rugby on TV1, 9 June 1991. A variant of 'everything but the kitchen sink'.

ex Former wife/husband or partner, often **the ex**.

extra Approving intensive, popular in phrases 'extra grouse' and 'extra curly' to mean something first rate or very attractive.

eyes like burn holes in a blanket Not looking well.

eyes on him/her like a stinking eel Pop eyes.

eyes out Maximum effort, such as 'going eyes out to win the race'.

eyes stick out like eggs in the wrong nest Very pop-eyed.

Face like a chook's bum

face like a bull's/chook's bum Ugly, dreary, drenched in misery.

face like a twisted sandshoe Image of disgust; eg 'One sip of port and the toddler had a face on her like a twisted sandshoe.'

face like an abandoned quarry Battered and ugly.

faces The answer to the pestering question what is for tea?

facial Roughing up the face of a tackled opponent, a rugby league forward habit of rubbing home the aggressive message; eg 'Kearney's been hammered, and he's copped a real facial.' Often observed by commentators but rarely by referees.

fag hag Female friend of male homosexuals.

fair buck/cow/dinkum/do/go Appeal for reasonable treatment, part of our egalitarian heritage.

fair crack of the whip/shake of the dice/suck of the saucestick/saveloy More extended appeals for fairness.

fair cow, a Unpleasant object or shabby act.

fakawi? Shortened form of the question 'Where the fuck are we?' The **fakawi bird** is invoked at parties as the herald of another rude repetitive chant, such as 'Long strong black pudding up my auntie's cat's pyjamas twice nightly' and 'I cumma zooming up your rectum'.

far canal Euphemism for 'fucking hell', an expression usually denoting exasperation.

fart sack Where you sleep etc.

farts like a motormower off its stroke/on the phut Flatulence of a staccato, uncontrolled nature.

fat Male erection. To **crack a fat** is to release it.

Father Christmas hold, the old The hand under the crutch of an opponent, inducing surrender. Commentator Keith Quinn called this in the All Blacks versus Swansea on 22 October 1989, adding 'rugby people will know what I'm talking about'.

fat show No chance.

feather to fly with, not having a Broke, or lacking prospects or any excuse, from a 'feather' meaning a farthing.

Featherston Street farmer Urban absentee farm owner, from a central Wellington business street.

feed a line Give somebody deliberately misleading information.

feel like a bagful of busted arseholes Not feeling well, as in one experiencing a hangover.

feel like a haunted shithouse Very hungover.

feel like a spare prick at a wedding Feel useless or unwanted.

fend off To take or steal.

Fernleaf New Zealander, from the fernleaf badge worn by soldiers in WWI.

fevver clucker Reversal of 'clever fucker' or smart aleck.

fill the tins Housewifely act of cake and biscuit baking.

financial Carrying cash or enjoying credit in the bank.

find another gear Competing person or animal that manages to make an extra effort.

finickity Fussy.

fire and flute Car heater and radio, developed as colloquial sales enticement in the days when they were not standard fittings.

fire in the fern Trouble brewing; eg 'It looks as though the stock market is stabilising. The fire in the fern, at least in regard to market leaders, is no longer there.' The phrase appears to have evolved out of Maori guerrilla warfare during the Land Wars, as characterised by W.P. Reeves in *The Long White Cloud*, London, 1898: 'Spreading from point to point, dying down and then starting up, it was as hard to put out as fire abroad in the fern.'

firefly Tent fly.

firing a warmer into the bank The first beer of the session.

firing blanks Failing to fertilise the female.

first-lettering Letting the first letter stand for the word as a way of disparaging it; eg 'You call that a car. It's a c!'

fish hooks Difficulties. The first thing politicians look for in any commissioned report.

fit as a buck rat In good physical shape.

fitter and turner Army cook, from alleged habit of cramming food into big pots and doing little more than stirring or turning the food.

fizz-boat A small, flimsy, noisy motorboat.

flag away Give something up, lose patience or confidence; eg 'C'mon, Col, let's flag this fishing lark away, we haven't had a bite in hours.' From the action of linesmen in rugby union waving their flags horizontally to indicate an unsuccessful kick at goal or a try not scored.

flakers Collapsed from too much alcohol, or simply sleeping over at somebody's place.

flapping like a dunny door in a high wind Panicky behaviour or compulsive talking.

flash a brown Expose the buttocks, to provoke others and/or amuse oneself and friends.

flash as a Chow on a red bike Ostentatious. A West Coast saying going back to the goldmining era, when a 'Chow' or Chinese man on a red bike was unlikely, for the Chinese kept a low profile.

flash your nasty A lewd request for a woman to expose her genitals.

flat stack/stick/strap/tack As fast as possible or maximum exertion.

flat to the boards Maximum effort.

flattie 1. Flat-dweller.
2. Punctured tyre.

flea taxi A dog.

flea track Parting in the hair.

Floater 1. A meat pie floating in gravy, popular at piecarts.
2. A turd that refuses to flush.

float-up A casual approach.

flog 1. To masturbate.
2. To steal.

flog off 1. To depart.
2. To sell something.

flog the log To masturbate.

flog your chops Talk incessantly.

flognosticate Thrash, as in 'I'll flognosticate you', usually a jokey threat to a wayward child.

flower in a wet spot Female on heat.

fluence Influence, usually in the phrase to put the fluence on. Earlier this century it referred to hypnotism.

fly cemetery Square cake containing dried fruit between slices of pastry.

flyblown Broke.

flying fox Rope declined across a gully or river with a container on a pulley attached so that boy scouts, adventure camp followers, trampers and other outdoors folk can slide themselves and equipment down the rope.

flying saucer A fried disc of sliced luncheon sausage.

fong Booze. 'To be fonged' is to be drunk, but 'to be fonged up' can also mean bewildered or bothered or in a mess.

footie Rugby union game.

footsteps on horseback Noisy kids.

for goodness' sakes, it's chicken flakes Exclamation, particularly if you have done something wrong, like knocking over a glass of milk. Derives from the chook on the cornflakes packet.

For years we've been led by a knight and kept in the dark Disenchanted trade union remark about longterm postwar president of the Federation of Labour Sir Tom Skinner.

freckle The anus.

freckle puncher Active male homosexual.

friend or enema? Jokey challenge to your loyalties.

frogs' eyes Boiled tapioca or sago.

frogs' eyes and onions Jokey response to 'What's for tea, Mum?'

frogs' tits and watercress Another answer to an enquiry about what is for tea.

frogskin Contraceptive sheath.

front bum Vagina.

froudacious Inaccurate. Obsolete term from combining 'audacious' with Froude's comments on this country about 1880.

fruit fly Female friend of male homosexuals.

fruit salad Mixed fishbait, such as pipi and trevally.

fuck a blind man's dog, would Said of a man considered extremely randy.

fuck-knuckle Idiot, but can be meant affectionately.

Fuck me dead said Foreskin Fred as he waved his wooden leg! Exuberant exclamation with no literal connotations.

fuck me dead with a bargepole! Another exclamation of surprise and positively no intention of being taken literally.

fuck me for a chocolate duck! Another exclamation without overtones or undertones. Nigel Watson recalls a friend using it as he emerged on deck and saw thousands of empty kilometres of South Pacific ocean.

fuck me sideways! Exclamation, often attracting the response: Not while there's cats.

fuck truck Any vehicle used for sexual trysts, often a panel van.

full as a bull/a Catholic school/a fairy's phonebook/a fart/a footy test/a goog (egg)/a Pommie complaint box/a seaside shithouse on Waitangi Day/a

tick Very drunk or full of food.

full tit Maximum output, usually from a car.

full up Exasperated, tired, disgusted.

full up to the dolly's wax So full of food one could not eat another morsel; from Victorian dolls having heads of wax.

Fuller's Earth New Zealand, from the Fuller theatres throughout the land.

fun bags Woman's breasts.

funny/silly as a piece of string Humorous.

funny money party Disparaging reference to Social Credit, which is believed to want to print money when it feels like it.

furburger Vagina as object of cunnilingus.

furburger and Y-bone Sexual meal, playing on the notion of a T-bone steak.

futuparu Rugby. A cod-Maori word.

fuzzy duck One of the Hokonui swindle type of drinking games students go in for. As this one progresses, it can be spoonerised or reversed to immense amusement of the drinkers concerned, the offender having to drain his glass.

FY boots Fuck you boots, the ankle-length variety that are part of tarty apparel along with tacky blonde hair and very short skirt.

Garbage guts

Gafu A monumental mess or mistake, acronym for 'God Almighty fuck-up', a WWII Kiwi soldiers' version of RAF's 'snafu', for 'situation normal, all fucked up'.

gangie/gangbash/gangsplash Serial rape, usually by a bikie gang.

garbage guts Greedy eater.

garbiologist Local version of a garbologist or dustman; eg 'RCA tells us of their local garbiologist.' *New Zealand Woman's Weekly*, 4 October 1965.

gark A nick or scratch; eg 'That table has a gark in it. Somebody's chisel slipped there.'

gate Mouth, as in 'shut yer gate, mate'. From about 1910.

Gawd pickle me nuts! Exclamation, usually of surprise.

g'day/g'die/gidday/gudday Kiwi versions of hello.

geek A look. From Cornish 'geek', an intense look.

gekko A look, combining geek and dekko, a look, from the Romany word 'dik', a look.

Gentle Annie A steep slope, hill or mountain, used by coachmen last century.

gerry An old person, as in 'geriatric'.

get, do a Run away, probably in a hurry.

get a boot out of Gain satisfaction; eg 'I really got a boot out of that,' a lawyer remarked of a client going straight in *Metro* magazine, March 1989.

get a milkshake Experience fellatio. Teenage slang.

get a shot away Achieve male sexual release.

get amongst it Enjoy engagement, usually sexual, but can be a booze session or making money.

get down on To steal.

get/give the runaround Treat evasively; eg 'Ever know a politician who didn't give you the runaround?'

get in behind! Jocular order to do as you are told, popularised by gumboot Kiwi comedian Fred Dagg, originally barked at sheepdogs to get behind the flock.

get off the grass! Scornful rejection. 'You become an All Black? Get off the grass!'

get off the train at Green Island/Papakura Coitus interruptus.

get on it To set about serious drinking of alcohol.

get out from under Extricate yourself from a difficult situation.

get out of it To become stoned on cannabis.

get out of jail Lucky; eg 'If the All Blacks win this they'll get out of jail.' Stu Wilson on the first test against Ireland, 30 May 1992.

get plunked Become pregnant, by association with the Plunket Society, which undertakes to care for pregnant women nobody else will.

get real! Emphatic way of telling someone to be realistic; eg 'Get real, Daph! That joker's never going to pop the question.'

get rooted! Rude rejection.

get stuck in/into To fight or engage vigorously in some activity.

get the old heave-ho/run Be given the sack; eg 'Bill was only there a week when he got the run.'

get the willies Become frightened or very nervous.

get to it! Command to engage in a task.

get your a into g/arse into gear Command to start doing something quick.

giggle house Mental institution.

gink 1. An idiot.
2. A person.
3. A look, in the phrase 'take a gink at'.

give a pop To fight; originally to fire a machine gun, among WWI Kiwi soldiers.

give curry To abuse or encourage aggressively, usually spectators wanting a better performance from a competitive sport.

give her/him a crispie! Reward someone, from the plain wine-style biscuit studded with sugar; eg 'Rudders finally got his century. Give him a crispie!'

give her/him a vibrator and tell her/him to buzz off Go away.

give it a burl/go/whirl Try something, often an encouragement to try.

give it away Abandon a project, often in defeatist fashion.

give it the wow, give it the matow
Give me a nail, give me a fish-hook
(matau), Maori pidgin as recorded by
J.L. Nicholas in 1814-15.

give it to the Belgians Advice to
somebody with leftovers or unwanted
goods. WWI Kiwi soldiers suggested
this solution first.

give jaro To scold, a bastardised version of Maori word 'wharo', to scold.

give jute To tease or criticise adverse-
ly.

give running shoes The sack.

give the go Reject a suitor or abandon
something, such as a place or a job.

glassy A glass marble.

glazing Sleeping with your eyes open,
or daydreaming. From 'glaze', eye or
eyesight.

glide time Public service initiative in
the 70s of working outside traditional
hours in a flexible fashion, trans-
formed by Roger Hall's play of the
same name into public servants skiv-
ing or slacking.

glory box Prospective bride's domestic collection.

gnawing Kissing the way streetkids
describe it.

go Agreement, often in the phrase it's
a go.

go and dunk your left eye in cowshit
Go away.

go and have a roll Go away.

go around with Steady relationship.

go bite your bum! Rude request to
absent yourself. Sometimes with the
ruder extension **and make sure you
leave your tongue in it**.

go down the toity To fail, 'toity' being
toilet; eg 'Maggie's goalshooting's
gone down the toity this season.'

go for a row of shitcans Be in big
trouble; eg 'That's his fourth drink-
driving offence. This time Jugsy'll go
for a row of shitcans.'

go for it Encouragement; eg 'C'mon,
Hakky. You've jumped that high in
practice. Go for it!'

go for the doctor To bet heavily on a
horserace or go as hard as you can,
take big risks, usually in some sporting effort. Probable West Coast origin
in the card game 'forty-fives', played
there since the goldrushes of the
1860s. Of Irish origin, it involved up
to five suits, with the top card the five
of the trump suit and cries of 'maggie', the ace of hearts, 'get jinx' and
'go for the doctor'.

**go home and ask Mum if you can go
to a wedding** Go away, you wimp.

go kiss a cocky's blowhole A rude
way of telling someone to get lost.

go like a hairy dog/goat Person or
animal moving very fast, or very slow.

go like a power of piss/shower of shit
Move fast; eg 'Once school is out,

that boy is off down the lagoon like a shower of shit.'

go like a strangled fart Move slowly.

go much on Approve of, usually in the negative, as in 'I don't go much on the new car registration stickers.'

go ninety to the dozen Travel very fast; eg 'Once he's in the clear, that winger Berryman goes ninety to the dozen.' The phrase lingers on long after imperial measure and longer after steam engines achieved top performance by pumping out 90,000 gallons for every 12 bushels of coal shovelled in. A Cornish saying that caught on here.

go off at To abuse.

go on the swag To become a tramp.

go out the bush To proceed into the bush; eg 'Dad, next time can I come when you go out the bush after pigs?'

go outside and tell your mother she wants you Dismissive remark.

go out with Keep steady company, or courting.

go the whole nine yards Complete a project by giving your all or receiving all you ever wanted. Often used of sportspeople who have put in a huge and successful effort. 'Nine yards' was Royal Air Force slang for 'everything' in the 70s, according to Partridge.

go to the pack To deteriorate.

go to whoa Beginning to end.

go up as high as Baldwin Get into trouble, as experienced by colonial balloonist Professor Baldwin; eg 'You nick one more bar of Black Forest chokky, Gran, and you'll go as high as Baldwin.' You can read about the high-flying prof in *Tales of the Colonial Turf* by John Scott.

go-ashore Three-legged iron cooking pot used by the pioneers.

goatboat Ski canoe or skiff, in surfie talk.

God Squad A clutch of committed Christians; eg 'Betcha those jokers comin' up the path in grey suits and white shirts are God Squad.'

God's gift to women A vain heterosexual.

God's waiting room Tauranga, 'because of its high proportion of superannuitants', wrote Richard Long in the *Dominion* newspaper, 23 September 1991.

Godzone New Zealand. Contraction of 'God's Own Country', which Thomas Bracken thought his best poem.

going jade An army jungle exercise.

Golden Kiwi State lottery that replaced the Art Union and was replaced by Lotto.

Golden Oldies Veteran rugby players who should know better but cannot resist pulling on the boots to play another team of grey hairs and dream of past glories and then get down to the real business of a drinking session to talk over who did what when to whom, on those golden rugby fields of yore.

Golden Shears International shearing and wool-handling championships held every March at Masterton since 1961.

goldie An impressive object.

goneburger Something departed, defeated or spent; eg 'A goneburger, as Stu Wilson would say.' Jim Hickey, TV1 weatherman, 15 May 1995.

goob/goobie Spittle or snot ball. From British dialect word 'gob', a slimy clot.

good fit, like a stocking on a chicken's lip Neat piece of work, in joinery a well-crafted job.

good ink Anything pleasing, as in 'What's the good ink on the latest Blues game?'

good leave, a Judicious action; eg commentator Glenn Turner called 'a good leave' when Ken Rutherford did not play at a Waqar Younis ball fast and rising outside the off stump, TV1, 20 February 1994.

good night, McGuinness! The end. Who McGuinness was is not known.

good night, nurse! Irrevocable turn of events. Beloved of our sports commentators; eg 'Intercept! Good night, nurse!' was Keith Quinn's call when the French began their match-winning try late in the test against the All Blacks, 3 July 1994. Earle Kirton used the same phrase when Australia made its match-winning move on the All Blacks in the 1989 Bledisloe Cup clash. The phrase originally was a WWI greeting the soldiers brought back from hospital, which developed into a comical or incredulous expression, and from about 1920, a phrase to mark the end or finish.

good old Kiwi ingenuity A self-congratulatory comment on New Zealand flair, often unconventional. Judy Bailey on the TV1 News, 10 August 1989, used the expression about a Christchurch couple with an exclusive contract from the Reserve Bank to destroy used notes, who proceeded to have them chewed up and used as lamp bases.

good-oh Excellent, or indicative of agreement.

good on you Well done.

good wicket Desirable state, as in 'We're on a good wicket with this fine weather.'

goody, goody, gumdrops Juvenile derision or enthusiasm.

goog 1. An egg.
2. A fool.

goolie A stone or rock on the West Coast.

goon Half-gallon; possibly a mishearing of the Australian 'goom', methylated spirits.

goori A dog, from Maori 'kuri'. Sometimes used as an abusive word for a person.

gorse-eater/goss-eater Ugly person, usually directed at a female by lower South Island males from perhaps the early 70s.

gorsepocket Mean person, often said to **have gorse in his pocket**.

goss 1. Gorse, usually in the southern South Island.
2. A gossip, as in 'Got any goss?' The ACT party obliges with a newsletter of parliamentary gossip titled 'The Goss'.

Gothic Dressed in tatty black, possibly dyed and spiked black hair. Punk fashion statement.

Grab and Snatch GST, or Goods and Services Tax.

graft Work, usually heavy manual labour.

grafter Willing worker or one trying his best.

Grand Scale Theft GST.

Granny Nickname for the *New Zealand Herald* newspaper, supposedly because it is old-fashioned.

grape Gang rape.

grape on, have a To be angry or sour at somebody.

grapes Haemorrhoids.

Grassgrub, the Railcars in Taranaki and South Island, from colour of cars.

graunch Loud grinding, often from failing to engage car gears.

greaser A heavy fall, often in the phrase **to come a greaser**.

greasies Fish and chips.

greenie A proactive conservationist.

grey matter Older people hired by young entrepreneurs to provide the illusion of an experienced operation.

greyhound A very thin self-rolled cigarette.

groppi mocker Best dress, from Groppi's hotel in Cairo frequented by Kiwi soldiers in WWII. They called the troops back at base **Groppi's Light Horse**.

grouse Desirable or excellent. Often applied to an attractive woman.

growler Vagina. Recent local extension of rhyming slang identifying 'cunt' as 'growl and grunt'.

grunds/grundies Underpants.

grunt Power, often horsepower; eg 'Boy, has that souped-up Holden got some grunt.'

grunter Promiscuous woman or prostitute, from the noise her male companion recognises or hopes to hear, from c1940.

gruts Underpants, a variant of 'grundies'.

Gumboot City Taihape, self-proclaimed and promoted in the 80s with a gumboot-throwing competition the Tuesday after Easter. A Taihape organiser of the Gumboot Day, Pamela Sykes, says the point of the exercise is to restore pride in a part of New Zealand's heritage whose neglect and ill-treatment – cruelly left on porches exposed to all weathers on their sides with wetas in residence – is a national disgrace.

gumdigger/gumpuncher A dentist.

gumdigger's dog, as mad as/as skinny as/as stupid as/as useless as Very mad/skinny/stupid/useless. In the case of skinny, **a gumdigger's bitch** is an alternative invocation.

gun Expert or admirable person. Originally a top shearer.

gunga Vagina or anus. Often used in the derisive suggestion 'stick it up your gunga'.

gurgler The plughole, often **down the gurgler**, indicating something is irretrievably lost or a complete failure.

gutbuster A mountain trampers know is going to be challenging.

gutless wonder Poorly performed person or thing; eg 'What a gutless wonder that new Number Eight turned out to be.'

guts for garters, I'll have your A threat.

guts, rough as An ugly or dishevelled person, perhaps from a night of excessive drinking.

guts, spill your To inform or tell all you know.

gutsache Irritating person.

gutser 1. Greedy person.
2. A significant failure, in the phrase **to come a gutser**.

gutsful More than enough, usually **to have had a gutsful**.

gutted Exhausted and/or disappointed. Increasingly used by rugby players interviewed after a game.

gutty Whitebait that has lived in freshwater long enough to no longer have a transparent gut.

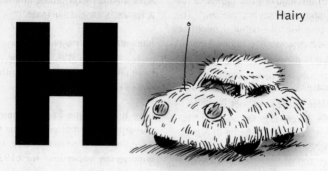

had it Complete exhaustion or complete exasperation, either relevant to 'I've had it with doing this GST.'

Hagley by day, Shagley by night Central Christchurch park allegedly changes at night to a place of sexual dalliance.

hair oil Worcester or other dark sauce, especially on the West Coast.

hair pie The vagina in cunnilinguist terms.

hairy 1. Rundown or of doubtful value; eg 'That's a pretty hairy motorbike you're trying to sell, Barry.'
2. Tricky; eg 'That new maths master comes up with some hairy equations.'

hairy legs The joker in the pack.

hairy maclary A female permitting sexual exploration but stopping short of connection.

half-caser The sterling coin worth half a crown or two shillings and sixpence.

half-g Large glass or plastic container for beer, which may no longer measure the half-gallon it means.

half-pie Unimpressive, poorly performed, not properly done.

half-rinsed Fairly drunk.

half the lies he tells you are not true Jokey way of saying someone is not a complete liar.

half-time Break midway through a sporting contest, formerly also the period after the shorts when there was time to buy refreshments before a feature film.

hand that lifts the cup, The/should not be used to shift the gears Advice not to drink and drive, especially farm machinery.

handle Beer glass with a handle.

hangi pants Hot pants, as in a female adjudged sexually on heat.

hangman Rough diamond.

hang of a/hanguva Mild intensive for those who avoid saying 'helluva'. The same goes for 'like hang'. I might say 'he is a hanguva good player', you might rejoinder, 'like hang he is.'

hard case/doer/shot/thing An amusing, exciting and/or resolute man or woman.

hard cheese Bad luck.

hard hitter Bowler hat.

hard word on, to put the A strong demand, for a loan, for sex, anything considered difficult to ask for.

hard yakker Demanding work, usually manual labour.

Harry twice Harihari, South Westland.

hash-me-gandy Sheep station stew. Possibly a combination of the restrained eater Mahatma Gandhi and/or the meat and egg mince called salmagundi.

hatchy malatchy, the world of Optimistic view that things are improving, expressed on *Holmes* TV show, 11 September 1989.

hatter Loner; from the goldmining era, his hat his only family, the loneliness sometimes making such men mad as hatters, who went mad from tanning hats with mercury.

have a hairy fit and die bald Extreme rage.

have a squat To defecate and also, in a female's case, to urinate.

have on To confront.

have one too many Overdoing the alcohol and showing it.

have the goods on In possession of damaging information; eg 'The police have the goods on that dealer who's winding back speedos.' NZ c1932, elsewhere later.

have the white gloves on Moving with authority, as traffic police did when directing traffic with white gloves; eg 'He obviously had the white gloves on – he was waving them through.' Comment from Arran Pene, TV1, on the opposition not tackling Eric Rush during the All Blacks game against a Scottish Development XV, 17 November 1993.

haven't laughed so much since Granny got her tit caught in the wringer Grossly amused, from the not unknown event in the days when washing machines had temperamental wringers attached, before built-in spin-drying arrived.

having a rottie Very bad mood, such as the image conveyed by the fierce guard dog breed of Rottweiler.

hay makes the bull fat, the bull makes the cow fat, the cow makes butterfat Kiwi response to 'Hey!', when polite people say 'I beg your pardon'.

he, I'll go Expression of surprise or vow of confidence; eg 'If that's not worth a fortune, I'll go he.'

head down, arse up Hard at work; eg 'Bolton's one of those jokers who works flat out dawn to dusk, head down, arse up.'

head job 1. Mentally lacking; eg 'Seth's a head job, couldn't add two and two together.'
2. Male oral sex; eg 'Ever noticed how popular head jobs are in American fiction?'
3. Ugly enough to need plastic surgery; eg 'Milt's got a face like a fright, needs a head job.'

head like a Mini with the doors open Sticking-out ears.

head like a twisted sandshoe Very, very ugly.

head over turkey Tipping over vigorously; variant of the army catchphrase 'arse over turkey'.

head read, need your Indication of doubts about your sanity or sense.

head sherang The boss. From Anglo-Indian 'serang', a captain or boatswain.

heads, I've seen better ... on a bumful of boils Indication of ugliness.

heady Clever, shrewd, full of ideas.

heap of shit Useless person or object; eg 'That car is a heap of shit.'

heap shit on Abuse or dismiss; eg 'That critic heaps shit on any local production.'

heaps, give her/him/it/them 1. Put or

demand extreme effort, as in ramming the accelerator to the floor of the car.
2. To tease or take to task.

heck and Thomas! Mildest expression of disgust.

Hector's birthday! Sardonic expostulation, referring to the resident parrot in Farmers Trading Company, Hobson Street, Auckland, store of yore and the perception that successive parrots were called Hector and Hector had birthday sales more than once a year.

he'd fuck a barber's shop floor if it had enough hairs on it Indiscriminately randy male.

hedgehog Radical feminist.

he'd go fuck a hole if it smiled at him Randy male.

heifer A woman; recorded by E.J. Wakefield among early C19th whalers here before elsewhere.

hell's bells and buckets of gravy Cute if pallid exclamation.

hell's bells and buggy wheels Mild exclamation.

hen cackle 1. A mountain that is easy to climb.
2. Any trifle.

hen fruit Hen's eggs.

hen's face A steep climb.

hen's teeth, scarce as A rare commodity.

hen's teeth, pickled eels' feet, pan petkin pie and Presbyterian custard One of the most elaborately arch answers to the unwelcome juvenile question 'What's for tea?' Popular in lower South Island.

Her/His Ex Short for 'Her/His Excellency, the Governor-General'.

herbs Power, usually motor power. Often in the phrase **give it herbs**. Originally oats for horses.

here's a go Anticipatory remark, as when spotting the potential for a rugby brawl.

here's looking up your kilt A popular toast.

hermit A sheep which has lost interest in being with the flock, as a result of being 'tuted', ie, eating the poisonous tutu plant.

he's a bigger ram than a Ramsden rammer rammer Said admiringly of a sexually active male.

hickey Thingummyjig, late C19th. Baker reported its use in the South Island, initially spelling it 'hiki', a Maori word one of whose meanings is a charm for raising anything from the water. Baker also offers 'do-hiki', very close to the American word 'do-hickey'.

hide Impudence or shamelessness. Often in **a thick hide**.

hide the sausage/soss Male intromission of the penis, or more generally, sexual intercourse; eg 'Fancy a bit of hide the sausage tonight, dear?'

high time Something just this side of overdue; eg 'It's high time you had yourself a holiday.'

highway robbery Excessive charging.

Hill, the Parliament buildings, adjacent to Hill Street.

hiss To tramp rapidly, usually in the phrase **to hiss along**.

hiss and a roar, with a Doing something obviously and/or loudly, with implication that you are maybe overdoing it. Some of the new Maori MPs in NZ First have entered Parliament with a hiss and a roar.

hisser Something welcome or admired, like a hisser of a meal.

hit around, a A social game, often of tennis; eg 'Let's use the lunch hour for a hit around, whadya say, guys?'

hit the sack Go to bed. A coal sack nailed to four posts was a cheap pioneering bed, still in use, as author witnessed in the done-it-himself abode of the late Tony Yelash, Ahipara's last gumdigger. The Royal Navy may have called a hammock a sack before or after Kiwis did. The Americans also hit the sack.

hit the spot To have precisely the desired effect, often from alcohol, but from any object of desire; eg 'Ooh, these oysters/James Lee Burke thrillers/cabsavs from Magill Cellars hit the spot.'

hit your straps Move or depart quickly. Possibly derived from looking for your swag-straps, which meant seeking another job.

hitimi A marble. Developed from 'hit me', the juvenile challenge in a game of marbles.

hobbles Form; eg 'Any French team — if it hits its hobbles on the day — can be impossible to beat.' Alex Wyllie quoted in the *Auckland Star*, 15 June 1989.

hockey sticks Hogget chops.

hoe in Vigorous effort, often in regard to eating heartily, originally related to gardening.

hoha Wearisome or wearied with expectation, importunity, anxiety, according to Williams' Maori dictionary. Keri Hulme writes that it is used extensively in modern Maori to mean a nuisance; eg 'You hoha thing!' or 'Somebody come and look after these hoha kids for a change.'

hoick To spit.

hokianga A mutton sandwich of doorstop girth.

Hokitika swindle Pub game involving numbers called in a certain sequence requiring a specified payment, used to purchase drinks.

hokonui Illegal booze, specifically the whisky made illegally in the Hokonui Hills of Southland.

Hokonui swindle Drinking game combining elements of chance with the ability to hold your liquor and follow a few simple rules. The deviousness of the caller can influence proceedings. The aim is fun, lots of drinking and seeing who can last the pace.

hold a tangi Experience problems or setbacks; eg 'We're holding a tangi with our kiwifruit farm. One more year like the last and we're stuffed.' Uses the Maori word for mourning.

holding Having ready funds. Often in the phrase 'Are you holding?'

holding paddock Old people's home.

hollow as a bunghole in a barrel Without credibility or simply quite empty, physically or metaphorically.

hollow log A dog.

hollywood Suspect or faked behaviour, often in the phrase **doing a hollywood**. Popular in competitive play to gain a breather.

Home Britain to previous generations, who referred to a Home boat, Home government, Home newspapers. The phrase **gone home** referred to worn-out clothes.

home and hosed Secure.

home on the pig's back Easy success or attended by good fortune.

homey Dismissive name for somebody who looks to Britain as home, or originates from there.

homogrips Sideboards.

hoo A bend or kink; eg 'That track's got a hoo in it.' Mostly South Island usage.

hoodackie Thingummyjig or object of indeterminate use.

hooer Abusive term, dialect or mock-Scottish for 'whore'.

ho-ohhh! Kiwi bushman's identification call, our version of 'cooee'.

hook one's bait/mutton Depart; eg 'As usual Fess only stayed in town the week, then hooked his bait.'

hool To drive fast.

hoon Hooligan. **Hooning around** usually means wild behaviour such as driving with squealing tyres and loud revving.

hooped Drunk.

hooray Farewell.

hoot/hootoo/hout/hutu Money, a corruption of Maori 'utu', ransom or price.

hoovering Consuming everything in sight, as the Hoover vacuum cleaner does.

hop to it To act speedily, or the command so to do.

hop up and down Distressed behaviour.

hopeye Hot meat pie, the nation's favourite lunchtime meal. The law requires it contain at least 25 per cent meat. In 1975 visiting US nutritionist Dr Walter Hodson described it as 'a few pieces of dead, overcooked meat and globs of gravy, fittingly entombed in a casket of white flour and grease'.

hophead Drunkard, or somebody acting silly enough to be thought drunk. To be **hopped out** is to be drunk.

hori A Maori, usually a male, a translation of 'George'.

horse cock Luncheon sausage roll.

hose in To win easily, often in sport.

hosed off Upset. Supporters are usually hosed off at their team losing.

hosing down Raining very hard; eg 'Boy was she hosing down the day we walked the Routeburn track.'

hospital pass A rugby ball passed to someone about to be tackled, anticipating where he will end up.

hostie Airline hostess.

hotten up one's copper Consume warm food or hot tea.

how about giving your feet a party and inviting your dress down? Your dress is too short, my girl.

how are you, now you're all right? Greeting that is not necessarily facetious or ironic.

how much would you charge to haunt a 10-room house? Indication you think someone ugly.

how would you be? Hello.

howleybags Nappies or knickerbockers, for slightly different reasons.

howsit goin?/how's she goin?/how ya goin? A greeting.

how's the way? Greeting earlier this century.

how's your bally knees/belly, knees and things? A friendly enquiry about your health.

how's your belly where the pig bit you? An enquiry about the health of your stomach.

how's your big wheel? An enquiry about the health of your heart.

how's your father A fight between rugby players; eg 'A little bit of how's your father in that scrum'. Keith Quinn on *Sportsnight*, TV1, 3 July 1990, attributed this meaning originally to D.O.C. Williams on a tour of South Africa in 1970.

hubberlush Desirable female. Variant of 'hubba hubba', from the mid-30s.

huckery Unwell or unpleasant. You could feel huckery, and you could see someone you regarded as huckery. Could be evolved from the Maori 'pakuru', ruined, via its corruption as 'puckeroo' and then 'huckeroo'.

Hughie 1. God, often in the phrase requesting rain, 'Send her down, Hughie'.
2. Mount Egmont/Taranaki.

hui-hopper Someone who spends all his/her time going to meetings.

humdinger Anything adjudged superb. It used to be applied to fast aircraft among American airmen, but here it refers to attractive objects.

hump To carry a load, from when swagmen humped their bluey.

humungous Huge; eg 'Snow just caught a humungous wave.'

hungry enough to eat the arse out of a dead horse/possum Very hungry.

huntaway A sheepdog that comes in from behind.

hurl To vomit.

hushytuttut On the booze.

hutch A crutch, from shearer's rhyming slang for crutch.

hydraulic sandwich A liquid alcohol lunch.

hydroglycaemic as a newt Drunk. A variant of 'pissed as a newt', inspired by a Member of Parliament in the early 80s claiming he was rendered tipsy by one beer on an empty stomach.

I don't give a fat rat

I beg your parding, Mrs Harding, that my chicks are in your garden eating all your cabbages Elaborately juvenile apology for a burp.

I couldn't care less if the cow calves or breaks its leg Indicative of extreme distinterest.

I didn't come down in the last shower Firm indication that someone is not to be considered a fool or naive.

I don't give a fat rat Indication of supreme indifference; eg 'I don't give a fat rat whether Fitzy plays or not, we will still win.'

I might as well speak to me bum – at least it talks back Protest at being ignored.

I visited New Zealand – it was closed A put-down of the country as dull. Among the visitors who have employed the remark was British Liberal MP Clement Freud.

ice Spotless; eg 'This room is ice. Nothing on the floor, no Barbie dolls, no rubbish.'

ickem Soft animal manure.

identity/old identity A person, usually one associated with a particular locality, or considered a dag or a wag or something of a character. Coined by E.B. Cargill in the Otago Provincial Council when he said settlers should endeavour to preserve their old identity amidst all these 1860s new goldrush identities. Popularised by Charles Thatcher in his goldfields balladeering about 'the old identities', the settlers there before the 'new chums' arrived on the goldfields.

if anyone can, a Kiwi can John Hanlon's 80s television ad catch-phrase for the Council of Recreation and Sport caught on, probably because it reinforced our self-image as resourceful folk.

if bullshit was music, you'd have your own orchestra Response to hearing a load of rubbish.

if bullshit was rubber, you'd fly to the moon You are talking rubbish.

if it moves, shoot it; if it doesn't, chop it down! Glum conservationist view of the way sportsmen and bushmen destroy native flora and fauna.

if it rained palaces, you would get hit on the head with the knob off the toilet door Very unlucky person.

if looks could kill ... Reaction to a frowning face, often intended to jolly somebody out of a moody, sometimes with the addition ... **I'd be dead.**

if that lump on your shoulders ever comes to a head, someone should squeeze it One way of expressing dislike.

if the missus of the house caught a mouse in her blouse would she rouse? – by Jove she would! Parental reaction to being pestered by children.

if you can't be good, be careful Advice to take precautions, usually with sex.

if you don't help yourself, nobody else will Advice to be self-reliant.

if you fell into a barrel of tits, you would come up sucking your thumb Unlucky person.

if you fell off the Arahura/Aratika/Maori/Tamahine, you'd come up with a mouthful of fish Lucky person, with reference to the unlikely fish-catch of someone falling off an interisland ferry.

if you had a brain, it'd be lonely You are stupid.

if you had a shit, your head would collapse A stupid person.

if you had another brain, you could start a rock garden Dolt!

if you laughed, your face would crack Morose person.

if you think that, then you've got another think coming You are wrong.

if you were side-on, you would be invisible A thin person.

if your brains were barbed wire, you couldn't fence a dunny You are stupid. Pre-WWII.

if your brains were shit, you wouldn't need any toilet paper No visible means of intellectual support.

if your head was full of dynamite, it wouldn't blow your hat off You are thick!

if you've got it, flaunt it Make use of your physical charms.

iffy Anything of dubious value or likely to be risky. Buying a secondhand car off the side of the road could be iffy.

Iky Ikamatua, West Coast.

I'll be eating ducks while you're chasing feathers Defiant boast that you will be more successful one day than somebody who is doing better than you now.

I'll fry your lips Warning to be quiet, hopefully a jocular one.

68

I'll hand it to him/I've got to hand it to him Expression of approval, perhaps reluctant; eg 'I've got to hand it to that forward pack, I never thought they could hold out the Blues for an entire half.'

I'll kick your bum and make your teeth bleed Threat, again hopefully jocular.

I'll punch your teeth down your neck until you fart them out A dire threat.

I'll see you right Promise to look after somebody, usually with some financial assistance; eg 'No worries about the mortgage, bro. I'll see you right.'

I'll trim the knots off you Promise of a thrashing; 'trim' is an old word for thrashing.

illegal tegel Any game bird shot out of season or any protected bird you should not be eating, such as the kereru, weka or muttonbird; after a popular brand of frozen chicken.

I'm not your bum boy I am not your servant.

I'm up stream with the trout Indication of intended imminent departure, with a caution not to enquire where.

improve, on the Sucessfully recuperating.

in a shit In sulky or petulant mood.

in deep shit In big trouble; eg 'We're in deep shit with spreadable butter

sales to the bloody Brits.'

in for your chop Vigorously working to get your share, or possibly more. From the divvying up of the sheep's carcase, from c1920.

in one ear and out the other Accusation of being inattentive, usually directed exasperatedly at a child; eg 'If I've told that boy once I've told him fifty times not to eat peas with his knife. Never listens. In one ear and out the other.'

in smoke In hiding, concealed, c1932.

in the dogbox In disgrace; eg 'Pete's in the dogbox with Madge after coming home pissed last weekend.'

in the poo In trouble; eg 'Monty gambles too much, he's always financially in the poo.'

in the shit In trouble; eg 'Looks like we're in the shit with this MMP carry-on.'

in two shakes of a dog's hind leg Promise not to take long; eg 'I'll be there in two shakes of a dog's hind leg.'

in you go, says Bob Munro Expression of encouragement.

in your dipper! Defiant expression; eg 'You want me to support Peters on this super tax scam! In your dipper!'

Inch and Pinch Peninsula of Gallipoli among the Kiwi soldiers in WWI trying to pinch an inch of it at a time.

Indian A Maori, in the early days. Borrowed from North American Native reference.

influence in the right quarter On the contrary, an ironic appreciation of a menial job such as latrine duty among WWI Kiwi soldiers.

Inland Robbing-you Inland Revenue Department.

Invergiggle Invercargill.

IQ below the room temperature Not too bright. David Lange identified somebody so on the sports chatshow *Boots 'n' All*, TV1, 15 June 1992.

IQ of a grapefruit Another identification of low-wattage in the brain box from the same show.

Irish confetti Gravel.

iron lung, wouldn't work in an Lazy person.

iron undies Any female garment adjudged difficult to penetrate or remove by coarse and frustrated males, including roll-ons, bicycling shorts, spandex tights, witch's britches, corsets, girdles, easies.

ironed out Exhausted or knocked senseless by fists or booze.

it/she couldn't drive a nail into a piece of balsa wood Poor quality car.

It's got to be good for you Champion miler and 1500 metre runner John Walker's television endorsement of an apple-based drink became a catch-phrase through the 80s for joggers and health-conscious consumers and anybody who wanted to make the point, even ironically.

It's in the bag! An army phrase for something easy to achieve or acquire was converted into the title of a radio and then a TV quiz show offering the winner a choice between the money and the bag. Original host Selwyn Toogood added his own catchcry 'What'll it be, customers?' The audience usually urged choice of the bag, which sometimes yielded the latest washing machine, sometimes a ballpoint.

It's the putting right that counts TV advertising avowal by whitewear salesman Alan Martin: 'If we've supplied it, we'll put it right. And if it's not put right, then ask for me, Alan Martin ...' Alan also offered money back if consumers could find a cheaper buy. Others use the phrase ironically to indicate a domestic appliance or other piece of machinery that has not been well maintained or serviced.

ittee ittee workee workee, ittee ittee kiki A little work and then some food, in Maori colloquial according to J.L. Nicholas in 1814-15; 'iti', small.

it was in Baghdad that you were in your dad's bag Your father was over there when you were conceived, but was your mother? More simply, you're a bastard.

it's a little bit over Reassuring remark from butchers and greengrocers and anybody else selling you more than you asked for.

I've been coming here 18 years in concussion Indication of confusion on the part of somebody being dim-witted. Alleged remark from Federation of Labour president Jim Knox, who had a reputation for stumbling over words.

I've been doing this since your arsehole was the size of a shirt button I am more experienced than you, with the implication that you should know your place and not criticise your betters.

I've got a carbuncle on my pollywonkle Facetious response, usually implying that it was a stupid question.

I've nearly bust my foofer/foofoo valve Indication that you have overdone the physical activity. The 'foofoo valve' was a mythical gadget blamed for breakdowns in the Royal Navy early this century.

I've read about you on jam tins Indication of doubt and suspicion of being deliberately misled. I don't believe you, you are kidding me.

I've seen better heads on a glass of beer You are ugly, my friend.

J

She's jake

jack A look, usually when you take or have a jack at.

jack of Rid of something annoying.

jack up 1. To organise, such as jacking up a date for the evening.
2. To support, as in jacking up a retaining wall.
3. Increase something, as in jacking up the price of fruit.
4. Organise deceit, as in jacking up a coalition deal.

jackberko A Central Otago quail, from the sound it makes.

Jackeytown Tiakitahuna pa, southwest of Palmerston North, in early Pakeha parlance.

Jacky Howe Dark sleeveless woollen working man's singlet, after a champion shearer.

Jafa Aucklander, in the acronym 'Just Another Fucking Aucklander'.

jaffa On the *Magic Kiwis* television series screened on 10 August 1990, Neil Roberts asked Richard Hadlee

what a jaffa was. 'The perfect delivery,' said the knight who bowled more of them than most anyone else in the history of the game.

jag To get on someone's nerves. Late C19th.

jagged Worn out, usually from hard tramping.

jagging Social visit, perhaps combining 'gad' or gossip and 'jag', a spree.

jake, she's Reassurance that everything is fine.

jam and butter it! Mild exclamation.

jandal Thong or flipflop, a spongy plastic or rubber sandal businessmen Morris and Antony Yock adapted from the geta or wooden Japanese sandal they saw in 1957.

Jap Japanese or sika deer, among deerstalkers.

Jap crap Cheap and nasty goods from Japan post-WWII, now dated.

jar Pint or handle of beer, or a jug of beer.

Jaybee Jungle bunny, originally Australian slang for a dark-skinned person, here a coastal hostess or ship girl, rendering sexual services to crewmen in exchange for travelling with them from port to port and accepting their gifts, sometimes acting as informant for Customs and Police in drug and other smuggling investigations.

jelly tip A Maori redneck, recorded the *Dominion*, 5 October 1993.

Jennycide Tough social implications of Social Welfare cuts imposed by then Minister of, Jenny Shipley, 31 March 1991.

jerkin the gherkin Male masturbation.

jerry To understand; eg 'We didn't jerry to their plans until it was too late.' Possibly from 'jerrycummumble', meaning to rumble or tumble to something. Also **full jerry**, to understand all the implications.

Jessie's dream Methylated spirits, a WWII term from Isaiah 11:1: 'And there shall come forth a rod out of the stem of Jesse.'

jigger Hand-operated railway line trolley used in line maintenance.

Jimmy Grant An immigrant. Whalers' rhyming slang.

Jimmy Woods-ing Solo drinking, especially used by miners. Said to be derived from an Australian loner, Jim Wood, in a poem of that name. Sometimes Johnny Woods-ing.

jingle Money. From c1925.

jingling johnnies Sheep shears. A shearer was a jingling johnny from c1870.

jink To cheat. From taking all the tricks in the card game 'forty-fives'. About 1920.

job in a spirit level factory, a Mildly derisive reply in lieu of the difficulty of explaining what you actually do.

joe 1. A person. From the goldfields warning of approaching police, often used derisively, hence
2. A foolish person, one who 'makes a joe of himself'.
3. A penny, c1935.

Joe Blakes The alcoholic shakes. Rhyming slang.

Joe Blow An ordinary bloke.

Joe Hunt A very foolish person, rhyming slang for 'silly cunt'.

john 1. Policeman, from rhyming slang 'John hop/cop'.
2. Chinese man, from goldfields habit of identifying all such as 'John Chinaman'.
3. Penis, shortened form of 'John Thomas'.

John Dory Signature, possibly rhyming slang for 'your story'.

joker A bloke.

journo A journalist.

judder bars Haemorrhoids.

jumbo Buttocks, from c1945.

jump-start Get a vehicle going with cables attached to another vehicle's battery.

jumper A cardigan. Originally a gold-miner's shirt, usually blue.

jungle hour Riotous domestic period around five until six pm, when young children go into feeding frenzy and frenziedly object to bath and bed.

junket around Act tiresomely, act the fool.

junket trumpet The penis in the context of its sexual employment.

just a mo/sec/tick Plea for a little more time, employing diminutives of moment and second, sometimes reduced to half a mo, sometimes varied to hold on a mo or hang on a mo.

just around the corner/down the street Very close in a variety of contexts. Good times, for instance, are said by politicians to be just around the corner.

just quietly Confidentially matey remark, as in 'Just quietly, Joel is a creep.'

just the berries Exactly what is wanted, perfect.

justin Half-gallon container of beer, just in case you run out.

Kaitaia

kai kart Piecart or fast food take-away that may or may not include kina with the chips. From the Maori 'kai', food.

kaitaia Takeaways or meals on wheels – the kai or food you take away on tyres, a splendid crosslingual pun.

kapaiburger Fresh white bread bun filled with beef pattie, slice of lettuce, onion ring, maybe beetroot, tomato sauce and mayonnaise made with condensed milk, possibly first served at Putaruru c1970. From the Maori 'ka pai', good!

kath An indefinite prison term, or any long period. From the words of the song Kathleen Mavouneen that parting 'may be for years and it may be for ever'.

keep your legs together Advice to young women not to make themselves sexually available.

keep your powder dry Advice to young men not to let drink spoil their sexual performance.

Kelliher art Dismissive phrase for chocolate box paintings of New Zealand landscapes, from the Kelliher Art Prize. Sir Henry Kelliher, Dominion Breweries founder, required entrants to paint a 'realistic or natural representation' of our country. The award ran from 1956 to 1977.

kerbstone jockey A relatively safe job. Originally WWI Kiwi soldiers' reference to the Army Service Corps.

kero Kerosene.

ket Electric kettle.

keyboard plaque Build-up of dirt and gunk on a computer keyboard.

kia ora G'day; Maori meaning 'good health'.

kick for touch Back off from a potential confrontation, resign from conflict. From the rugby union action of kicking the ball across the sideline, often to get out of a threatened defensive situation.

kick her/it in the guts 1. Expression of doubt; eg 'Ya reckon there's gold in that creek. Kick her in the guts, mate. I didn't come down in the last shower.' 2. Advice to be more aggressive, perhaps use brute force to get an activity or machine under way.

kick him where his mum never missed Disciplinary prescription, usually aimed at the testicles, sometimes the buttocks.

kick on To continue, often successfully; for example, a 1500 metre runner may surge through the field, kick on and win the race.

kick up bobsydie Cause trouble by being aggressive, making a lot of noise.

kicking tyres Discussing vehicles.

kiddo A girl, from late 1880s.

kidney buster/crusher/rider/rotter/ sweater A frameless backpack that bounces into the kidneys of a tramper.

kidney pie Insincere praise, from early this century, from the Antipodean habit of kidding or teasing or deliberately misleading for the fun of it.

kin oath Rude reassurance, short for 'fucking oath'.

kindy Kindergarten, from c1950.

King Country spanner Bottle opener.

king fleece/mate/tide/tree, etc Any object rated tops, though not always

with approval; eg 'She was a king tide last night. Thought the house was going to get swept away.'

king hit Knock down or maybe knock-out blow, c1920, and latterly any sudden misfortune.

kingfisher, kingfisher, take my luck Children's chant urging a stationary kingfisher to fly off, thereby bringing rather than taking luck.

kiss-crust Two loaves of bread baked in the same tin and pulled apart when done.

kiwi, a definition: A nocturnal creature that eats, roots and leaves, or eats roots and leaves. The comma makes all the difference between the sly Kiwi seducer and the shy threatened native bird that has become our national nickname.

Kiwi fruit A New Zealand homosexual.

Kiwi green Cannabis grown in this country.

knockabout Handyman. A sheep station worker from c1875, expected to turn his hand to many tasks.

knock back To reject, or a rejection if a hyphenated noun, knock-back.

knock down 1. To drink alcohol greedily or live indulgently. 2. To introduce somebody, in the compound form to give the knockdown.

knock it on the head Curt demand to be silent; eg 'Knock it on the head, will ya. There's a kid tryin ta sleep in the next room.'

knock up 1. To make pregnant.
2. To make something readily, such as a batch of scones.
3. To wake somebody.

knocks like a ten-ton lorry Sexually aggressive woman.

knocker Punctual, in the phrase 'on the knocker'.

knuckle-up A fist fight.

komaty Dead. From the beginning of Te Rauparaha's famous haka, 'ka mate', 'it is death'.

kotanga Car aerial, a pun on 'coathanger', which is sometimes twisted out into a diamond shape and employed as an ad hoc car aerial.

kumara cruncher A Maori.

Laughing gear

L&P Lemon and Paeroa, a popular soft drink made originally from Paeroa mineral water.

ladies a plate The traditional covered plateful of savoury or sweet food women were expected to contribute to a gathering, while the men brought flagons of beer and maybe bottles of sherry for the ladies.

lady's leg Liqueur bottle, from the shape of its neck as much as any male expectation.

lamb-brained Weak or stupid; eg 'That's a lamb-brained notion you have, cross-leasing a section that small.'

Land of the Long Black Cloud/Long White Shroud/Wrong White Crowd Jocular variations on 'Land of the Long White Cloud', the popular translation of Aotearoa.

land with your bum in butter Excessively lucky.

lanny Land Rover, a four-wheel-drive vehicle.

larrikin A thug or a high-spirited youth.

lash An attempt, usually in the phrase **to have a lash at.**

laugh on the other/wrong side of your face Crying, or miserable; eg 'If that brat keeps pulling her pigtails, he'll soon be laughing on the other side of his face.'

laughing gear The teeth or mouth. Barry Crump invited viewers to 'wrap your laughing gear around this' as he handed over a fish in a 1987 television ad.

lay a cable Void the bowels.

lay an egg 1. Make a fuss; eg 'No need to lay an egg, we'll have your electricity back on in a minute.' 2. Void the bowels.

layby Item secured by a deposit, different from hire purchase in that no interest is paid, but the item is not uplifted until the full cost is handed over. Popular arrangement with department stores.

leather lady Possum after a train or vehicle has flattened it.

leftfooter A homosexual.

legs like a Tokoroa forest Very thick, very hairy legs.

lekker/lekkers Electricity.

lemon-lipped Demonstrably irritated.

lemon squeezer Former Kiwi army hat that looked so.

length The penis, particularly when tumescent; eg 'Get your length in last night, Jock?'

let her rip Advice to get something going, often a vehicle.

let me chat you! Desire to impart information, WWI Kiwi phrase.

let the hare sit Advice to relax.

lezzo A lesbian.

lick An ice cream, from the teen 60s.

lick at the cat and a run round the table Frugal meal.

lie down and I'll fry you an egg Sarcastic response to an unreasonable request.

lie like a flatfish on Riverton Beach Lie extravagantly.

like a daisy in a bull's mouth Tasty morsel.

like a dog golloping tripe Noisy sexual activity.

like a fart in a fit Agitated state.

like a fart on a curtainpole In a hurry.

like a hawk in an onion sack Very uncomfortable.

like a hooer at a christening Confused state.

like a maggot on a hot plate Fidgety.

like a mushroom – kept in the dark and fed on shit Not kept informed and not happy about it. **A member of the mushroom club** indicates someone excluded from what is going on.

like a pimple on a pumpkin Insignificant.

like a rat up a drainpipe Quick moving, often in pursuit of sexual gratification.

like a stunned mullet Stupid or dazed.

like having a shower with your raincoat on Wearing a condom.

like it's going out of fashion Very fast; eg 'That joker spends money like it's going out of fashion.'

like kissing your sister Dull; eg 'That second test was dead boring. Like kissing your sister.'

like pushing butter uphill with a hot needle Not easy.

like pushing shit uphill with the end of your nose Not easy and not pleasant.

like shagging a bag of nails Unpleasant sexual intromission.

like shit to a blanket Sticky and unpleasant.

like shitting in bed and kicking it out with your teeth Gross.

like talking to a brick wall Somebody not listening.

Limited, the Passenger train on the Main Trunk Line, so-called because it had a limited number of stops.

line A flirtation, in the phrase **to do a line with.**

lip like a motherless foal Sulky.

lippie Lipstick.

lips are sealed, my I can keep a secret.

lips like string Lips clamped thin in anger or distaste.

liquid amber Beer.

liquid laugh A puke.

liquid lunch Alcohol only.

little beaut/ripper Excellent person or thing.

little house, the The toilet.

Little Italy Island Bay, Wellington, because of its strong Italian community.

little lady, the The wife.

little pigs have big ears Warning that children may be listening.

littlie An infant.

live off the fat of the land Enjoy a comfortable life.

live off the land Feed yourself from what you can shoot or harvest.

Log, the/Log o' Wood The Ranfurly Shield, interprovincial rugby trophy named after the much-admired, turn-of-the-century Governor of New Zealand, the Earl of Ranfurly.

log of wood Stupid or lazy person.

logs, the Lock-up or small prison made quickly from logs, a goldrush necessity in the 1860s.

lolly A sweet; shortened form of 'lollipop'. A **lolly scramble** is a tossing of lollies into a group of children or the political promise of goodies to a supposedly corruptible and probably naive group of voters, quite different from **chucking/losing/tossing your lollies**, which means to vomit, **doing your lolly**, which means losing your temper, or a **lolly night**, the expectation of sexual fulfilment on pay day. **Lolly water** is a soft or insipid drink.

long acre/paddock The verge, where animals get free grazing.

long john 1. Outdoor dunny, where

long johns or heavy underwear had to be divested.
2. Oblong loaf of bread.

long-handled shovel Banjo.

long tall streak of weasel piss Lanky person.

long time looking at the lid Dead for some time.

long-distance call on the big white telephone Vomiting into the toilet bowl.

looks like the back end of a cow Ugly.

looks like the scum off a Chinese pisspot Scungy-looking food.

looks like two ferrets fighting in a sack Large person's rear.

loopie A tourist, who travels in a quick loop and then is off. A dismissive term.

loosie Loose forward, or the open side and tight side flankers and Number Eight at the back of the scrum in rugby union, compared to 'the tight five' forwards.

Lotto The weekly national lottery, which it is a contraction of.

lounge bar Private bar in hotels where people get to sit, where ladies were allowed when they were not in the public bars before the 70s.

lower than shark shit Despicable.

luck of a Chinaman Very lucky, enjoying good fortune, sometimes implication you do not deserve it.

lug-punch A natter with a friend.

lunatic soup Alcohol.

lunch box The bum. To open your lunch box is to fart.

lungbuster Cigarette.

lurk A sham or smart plan or cushy job, often in the phrase **on a good lurk**.

lux To vacuum, short for the Electrolux vacuum cleaner. With a particular attachment you can **lux the Venetians**.

Maggot pack

mad as a maggot Very silly or eccentric.

mad as a Maori on a motorbike Wild. Early C20th phrase no longer used.

mad as a meataxe Very silly or angry.

mad-dog To pester persistently, as offspring are wont to with a busy parent.

mad money The English girl's return fare, either from a colonial soldiers' party or the colony she had been lured to by a soldier or boyfriend who subsequently proved unreliable.

madwoman's shit, all over the place like A mess.

maggot pack Meat pie.

maggoty Unwell or irritable, c1915.

magic word, the The required comment, usually the word 'please'; eg 'You don't get a sweetie until you say the magic word.'

magpie A thief, to the WWII Kiwi soldiers who had somebody taking

their tobacco or soap or whatever without asking.

Magpies, the Hawke's Bay provincial rugby team, from their black and white playing colours.

maimai Any makeshift shelter, often a duckshooters' hide. From an Aboriginal word 'miamia', but not in use in Australia.

Main Trunk The main railway line between Auckland and Wellington, and sometimes its continuation from Picton to Dunedin or Invercargill.

Mainland, the The South Island.

make a box of Make a mess of something.

make a break 1. Run from the police. 2. Cut through the opposition in a game of rugby.

make a kai Prepare a meal, among Central North Island forestry workers.

make a sale To vomit.

make your marble good To improve your position, as you attempt to do in the game of marbles.

makings Roll-your-own materials, the loose tobacco in a pouch with cigarette papers.

mallowpuff Maori Maori academic achievers, as perceived by school peer group.

malt sandwich Glass of beer.

mango Kiwi $50 banknote, from its orange colour.

mango tackle Head-high tackle.

mangy Mean-spirited.

Maori bunk A bed shared by several people.

Maori chief Kiwi fish which looks as if its head has been tattooed.

Maori foreplay Are you awake?

Maori kisses Kiwi biscuits using cocoa, milk, butter, flour, sugar and baking powder.

Maori Magna Carta Early term for the Treaty of Waitangi that could catch on again.

Maori overdrive Coasting your car downhill in neutral gear.

Maori PT Taking it easy when you should be hard at exercise, used by WWII troops as a variant of Egyptian PT.

Maori pyjamas Marijuana.

Maori roast Fish and chips or a pie and a jug of beer.

Maori screwdriver Hammering the screw in with a hammer.

Maori sidestep Barging straight into somebody.

Maori splice Any quick and effective way to save hours of work, like splicing an eye in a wire rope.

Maori strum Defined by the Crowded House singer/songwriter Neil Finn as 'that chinga chinga pub sound, it should be in a dictionary', on the programme *Noisy Neighbours*, TV2, 26 November 1992.

Maori time Easygoing, unconcerned about time.

Maoriana European ceramics featuring Maori imagery, such as a cute little marae version of a weather-cottage, made in the 50s and 60s for the tourist trade.

mare and foal Bankroll.

massive! Exclamation of considerable approval.

mate Companion or partner, often used affectionately in the phrase 'me old mate'.

mate's rates Preferential charges.

MDO A sickie, as in **Maori Day Off**.

mean, so ... he/she wouldn't give a rat a railway pie/piss on you if you were on fire/wouldn't give you the steam off his shit Restrained in his or her generosity to the point of being financially challenged.

meatbeater Male masturbator.

member of the Wandering Hands Society A man or woman who fondles another sexually without asking.

metho Methylated spirits addict.

Metho Methodist.

michael/mick/mickey/mickeydidi The vagina, transposing the English meaning of a penis.

michael-muncher/minge-muncher Cunnilinguist.

Mickey Do/Doolan A Catholic.

mid-air passenger exchange Collision between planes in flight.

Middlemore pass Rugby ball passed to a player about to be crunched in a tackle that could well put him out of the game and into Middlemore, an Auckland hospital.

midgic Shilling; obsolete.

Mighty Totara The mostly Maori term of respect for someone; when Prime Minister Norman Kirk died in office in 1974, it was said the mighty totara had fallen.

millionaire's salad Nikau palm heart, a delicacy.

mind your own beeswax/duckhouse/ fowlhouse Mind your own business.

mingie A person who is twice a miser, both mean and stingy.

Minto bars Police long batons during the 1981 anti-Springbok Tour protests, when these batons were introduced to control crowds led by John Minto, spokesman for HART, Halt All Racist Tours. Play on two popular confectionery lines, Minties and milky bars.

miserable as a shag on a rock Very depressed.

miseryguts A complainer.

MMP Make More Politicians/ Mega-Mix Puzzle, jokey versions of Mixed Member Proportional Representation, the new New Zealand political system from 1996.

moistie A desired woman.

moleskin squatter Small sheep farmer, from the moleskin trousers he used to wear.

Mondayitis The blues at the beginning of the working week.

Mongy Mongrel Mob gang member.

monte/monty A sure thing, or something superlative. A tipster will assure you a racehorse is a monte, while you might call somebody who has helped you a monte. Derived from the three-card monte trick in a card game imported from America with the gold-rushes.

Monzter, the Disapproving nickname for the new concrete Museum of New Zealand being built on reclaimed and abandoned wharf land in Wellington at a cost at last count of over $300 million.

mood adjuster A few beers.

Mooloo Pantomime cow mascot of Waikato provincial rugby team.

mopey as a wet hen Glum and aimless.

more arse than class More energy or luck than intelligence or style, but doing well; eg 'That new bantamweight has more arse than class.'

more cheek than a fatman's arse Impertinent person.

more front than Milne's 1. Cheeky. 2. Large-breasted woman. Both refer to Auckland's Queen Street department store of yore.

more jungletime than Tarzan A soldier who has served a long time in the front line; army slang from Asian service.

more money than a bull can shit Very wealthy.

more strife than a pregnant nun More trouble than something is worth.

Morepork, the North Auckland train distinguished by its melancholy whistle.

morning glory Tumescent penis first thing.

mosher Crowd surfer; somebody who gets so excited at a rock concert he or she climbs over the crowd gesticulating wildly, perhaps disrobing.

mossie Mosquito.

mother-in-law's kiss, colder than a Unfriendly.

mountain mop The plant *Dracophyllum traversii* that Canterbury trampers use to clean pots and billies.

mountain oyster Sheep testicle, a delicacy for some.

mountain trout Early settlers' name for the kokopu or cockabully, *Galaxias fasciatus*, a small freshwater fish related to whitebait.

mousetraps in your pocket, to have Mean with money.

mouth like a torn pocket A gossip or plain ugly mouth.

mouth like a yard of elastic A gossip.

mouth like the inside of a Pommie's jockstrap Rank, fuzzed taste from too much booze the night before.

move out To develop. Most seasons a new All Black like Christian Cullen moves out or expands his game.

mower's blight Ringbarking or killing park trees by careless use of a motor mower or similar machinery.

mudguard Bald head, sometimes with the accompanying phrase **shiny on top, all shit beneath**.

mudguts Fat person.

mudhook A hand, c1915.

mullet, like a stunned In a dazed state.

mullock Rubbish. Poking mullock was teasing or jeering. **To mullock over** was to shear badly.

multi Multi-millionaire. Popular in Auckland.

mum and dad Mad; a rhyming slang acronym and perhaps a Freudian explanation for madness.

munga/munja Food or a rest break. Army slang, possibly derived from French 'manger', to eat. Rations among WWII soldiers were 'the munja party'.

munted Destroyed, defeated, wiped out.

murder house School dental clinic.

muso Musician, usually of the rock music variety.

muster an easy beat Enjoy a comfortable job, originally army use.

mutant Idiot; popular with teenagers.

mutton-fish Paua.

muttonflaps Woman's genitalia.

muttongun Penis.

my arse is a red cabbage Reassuring phrase; eg 'If that is not true, my arse is a red cabbage.'

my bloody oath/my colonial oath!/my oath! Exclamations of affirmation.

my heart pumps custard Sarcastic pretence of sympathy; eg 'I hear Smithy's down to his last six mill. My heart pumps custard.'

My Vehicle Disappeared Instantaneously Jokey version of MVDI, Motor Vehicle Dealers Institute.

mystery parcel Meat pie; also in expectation of surprises, like a used sticking-plaster, preferably not in the meat pie.

N

To lose one's nana

nail Rustbucket of a car.

nail your hide to the dunny door
Threat of a thrashing; eg 'If that kid spits one more time on the floor, I'll nail his hide to the dunny door.'

naked lady Pink lily.

nana Head, popular in the phrases **to do/lose one's nana**, to lose your temper.

narg An Indian.

nark To annoy or to be annoying or a spoilsport.

nasty Vagina.

Nat Member of the National Party.

naughty Sexual act.

NBG No bloody good; eg 'NBG to that idea, Frosty. You'll have to come up with something better if you want to keep your job.'

nearly die laughing Lengthy laughter to the point of being painful; eg 'Sir Les was so funny I nearly died laughing.'

nearly had a fit/heart attack/heart failure/kittens/jumped out of my skin/pissed myself/shat myself/wet myself/went down the tubes/went for a burton, etc Antipodean habit of experiencing almost-shocks, often in the course of relating an anecdote featuring the narrator; eg 'There I was, going on about her op in the hairdressers, Darlene nodding and winking and seeming a bit twitchy, then who should emerge from under the drier? Yeh, right, you can imagine how I felt. I nearly had a fit/kittens/wet myself' etc.

neat/neat,eh?/neato Pleasing. 'Like my jumper? Neat, eh?'

ned Two heads in a game of two-up; from Edward VII or Ned having his head on one side of the penny.

neddy Racehorse. **Off to the neddies** is off to a day at the races.

need a good kick up the arse/bum/khyber, etc In need of disciplining; eg 'That Pycroft brat needs a good kick up the bum before he gets completely out of control.'

Nelson huntaway A rock rolled down a hill to move sheep instead of using a huntaway, the mustering dog.

nervous as a newborn kitten in a room full of Rottweilers Very nervous.

nervous burger Cigarette.

nest of sparrows flew out of me arse, a Expression of deep sexual gratification.

new chum New arrival, particularly on the goldfields, where it was a dismissive term for a greenhorn.

new chum's gold Fool's gold.

new iniquity Immigrant, specifically to the goldfields.

New Zild New Zealand.

next bloke, the Average person; eg 'I did find the wallet, officer. Fair go. I'm as honest as the next bloke.'

Nga bush Nga Puhi tribe.

Ngati Blow Ngati Porou tribe.

Ngati DB Maori beer drinkers.

Ngati Drongo Not our tribe. Those Ngati Drongos are claiming the moon.

Ngati Irish Waikato tribe, in recognition of their taste for debating injustices they have suffered.

Ngati Pakeha Europeans.

Ngati Walkabout D Company 'was known as the Ngati Walkabout'. *New Zealand at War*, TV1, 9 May 1995.

nick, in good Rude health or fine physique.

nick, in the Nude.

nick away To depart, quickly and/or surreptitiously.

nick out Leave quickly.

nick over Visit a neighbour or friend.

night's a pup, the Early still, too soon to stop whatever.

Nimby factor, the Not in my backyard; Paul Holmes used it of Bay of Plenty objectors to a proposed drug and alcohol centre at Pikowai, on his show, 1 March 1990.

ningnong Idiot.

Nippon Clipon The Auckland Harbour Bridge, from the Japanese-made outer lanes added later.

nips on, to put the To ask for a loan of money. You can also put the nips in, or the squeeze on.

no beg pardons Full and vigorous and often aggressive commitment, often in sport.

no brain surgeon Not too bright; eg 'The kid's hard-working and reliable, but he's no brain surgeon.'

no fear! Expression of refusal or lack of agreement.

no-hoper A failure, either person or racehorse.

no sense in sticking your nose in butter if you're going to have to eat dripping the rest of your life Discouraging advice against dressing or acting above the station in life you are condemned to.

no tokee, no tokee, no porkee, no porkee No iron from you, no pork from us; pidgin English by Maori, recorded by J.L. Nicholas, c1815; 'toki', Maori for axe or tool.

no worries Reassuring remark. 'No worries, mate, we'll make it.'

no wucking furries No fucking worries, I can handle it.

nob Double-headed penny useful for cheating in the betting game of two-up, from the word for 'head'.

nobbler Dram or measure of spirits last century.

nobody home Not very bright or not concentrating, often with blame implied, as in 'The winger ran straight round the fullback, who just stood there, like there was nobody home.'

noggin 1. The head.
2. A glass of beer.

nohi Unacceptably inquisitive. Often Jack nohi, from Maori 'kanohi', the face.

nong Fool. Of Aboriginal origin.

North Cape to Bluff Complete coverage of the country.

North Sea rabbit Herrings among Kiwi soldiers WWI.

nose, a bit on the Protesting unfairness.

not a dog's show No chance; eg 'You haven't got a dog's show of jumping two metres.'

not having a brass razoo Without any money.

not know your arse from your elbow Confused or naive or plain dumb.

not much chop Unimpressive. A backfiring car could be considered not much chop.

not really Evasive denial, often ironic; eg 'You're asking me if I can meet the shortfall? Not really.'

not the full quid Mentally disadvantaged.

not too foul Quite nice; eg 'This lowcal beer's not too foul, eh?'

not worth a cracker/a cuntful of cold snow/a pinch of possum shit/a row of shitcans/a tin of fish/two knobs of goatshit Some of the ways in which something is declared useless.

nuddy Euphemism for nude, often in the phrase 'in the nuddy'.

nuky Manuka scrub.

number eight 1. A thick-gauge fencing wire that is used for many other quick fixes.
Sometimes used jokingly to indicate an ad hoc solution, as a doctor suggested he might use to a patient after an operation came unstuck. Not to be confused with
2. The forward at the back of the rugby union scrum.

nut, the The rugby union ball.

nut them!/nutted 'em! Exclamation when the pennies both come up heads in the game of two-up.

O

Ocker/Aussie

OB Outer board, the softer wood borer leave their tracks in, which they do not in heartwood.

Ocker/Aussie An Australian.

OE Overseas Experience, which young Kiwis get, often on a working holiday. John Muirhead coined the phrase in the early 70s.

off like a bride's nightie/a larrikin's hat in a high wind/a robber's dog/a whore's drawers, etc Swift departure.

off they go, says Bob Munro The mysterious Bob Munro again, this time signalling the start of something, like a race or the divesting of clothes preparatory to sex.

off your face Stoned, usually on marijuana, but also booze and other drugs.

offside 1. In someone's bad books. 2. Ahead of the play in rugby, thereby guilty of an infringement.

offsider Assistant. Rugby coaches often have them, as do chefs.

oh, bloody good, whacko, Pup! Exultant exclamation from Kiwis in WWII at some achievement such as downing an enemy plane.

oh how many cows live in Otaki? Ohau, Manakau, Levin, Otaki – chanted quickly.

oil, the/the dinkum oil/the good oil The inside information.

oily rag, live on the smell of an Very poor.

olds Parents, adults.

on a bad run/trot Period of misfortune.

on a good run/trot Period of good fortune.

on it/the bash/the scoot Drinking spree.

on the bones of your arse/bum Destitute or ruined; eg 'The national lacrosse team's on the bones of its bum. It can only go up from here.'

on the outer Excluded from the group, ostracised; eg 'Ever since Barbara blabbed to the teacher, she's been on the outer.'

on the turps Boozing heavily.

on the up Improving health following illness or injury; eg 'How's that flu? On the up?'

on your ear 1. Drunk, c1910.
2. Something easily accomplished, c1920; eg 'That kid can do the most complicated computer games on his ear.'

on your pat On your own, in the rhyming 'Pat Malone'.

once more round the gasworks Call for one more effort.

one brick short of a load Mentally challenged.

one for the pot Extra spoonful of tealeaves, often in the phrase, 'One for you, one for me, one for the pot.' Can be used to promote extra generosity.

one for your duckhouse roof A setback or snub. Derives from the Australian habit of chalking up a score on the duckhouse roof or wall, denoting a delay or defeat. Out of use there since c1910, according to Partridge.

one look is enough Indication that you are not impressed, or highly impressed; eg 'One look was enough, I bought the car there and then.'

one out of the box An outstanding object or achievement, such as a spectacularly fine day.

one sheep to the acre 1. Steamed currant pudding that is very short on currants, from the consumer's perspective, often in a boarding school context.
2. Not very bright person.

one-eyed trouser snake The penis.

only nineteen shillings and sixpence in the pound Not all there in the mental department.

oodle Money.

oozle To obtain illicitly or by scheming. From WWI troops.

op shop Opportunity shop, selling secondhand goods very cheaply.

OPC Other people's cigarettes, usually requested by someone giving up cigarettes and not having any on them but desperate at the sight of another person smoking, or merely spotting someone's fags.

open out 1. Bad behaviour.
2. A game of rugby that becomes free moving.

open slather No constraints, a free-for-all. Maybe Irish 'slighe', access.

open-collar workers People who work at home and most likely communicate by computers.

orchestrated litany of lies Official whitewash, or anything perceived as less than the truth, from Justice Peter Mahon's sceptical 1981 phrase for the bureaucratic evidence placed before his inquiry into the crash of an Air New Zealand DC10 into Mount Erebus, Antarctica, with no survivors of this tourist flight.

ordinary bloke/joker The only partly apocryphal average Kiwi full of modesty and resourcefulness.

Oriental Parade The well-to-do of Wellington, who live in the ritzy inner suburb of Oriental Bay; eg 'Cable Street New World is a well-known gathering place for the well-to-do, or Oriental Parade.' *The Dominion*, 4 July 1995.

Otahuhu sidestep No sidestep at all, but a battering ram approach to taking the rugby ball forward; eg 'Otahuhu sidestep – straight into him.' Graham Lowe on *Aussie League on Two*, 10 April 1994.

Other Side, the Australia, from c1880.

Otira tunnel Sexually available woman on the West Coast, which you enter through the Otira tunnel.

OTT Over the top; eg 'That new actor on *Shortland Street's* OTT, darling.'

our muttons Some person or thing highly regarded; eg 'Ian Jones should've been captain years ago. He's just our muttons.'

out of your tiny mind Your stupidity comes from your impressively small mind.

out on its own, like a country dunny/shithouse Unique, but not necessarily admirable.

out the back The toilet; eg 'Sorry, madame, but at this bach you have to go out the back.'

out the back door Where Kiwi soldiers went, down the beach at Gallipoli in WW1, mostly on fatigues.

out to it Unconscious from excessive alcohol.

outer Rejected, often in the phrase 'on the outer'.

over the fence Unreasonable, greedy, outrageous, akin to being beyond the pale; perhaps a reference to hitting a cricket ball over the fence for six.

over the shoulder boulder holder Bra, c1935.

overstayers People staying here illegally after work permits expired; usually Pacific Islanders.

oxygobblers Old people, as perceived by callous kids, as people gobbling up oxygen and little else.

OYO Own your own, usually a self-contained flat.

P

Pack a shitty

pack, to go to the To deteriorate, including the process of continuous deterioration. Many a public building in New Zealand has been allowed to go to the pack, in order that such a sorry structure may be demolished without much protest.

pack a sad Displaying a deficiency or depression. From the building term for a warp or sag in a wooden structure.

pack a shitty To lose your temper; eg 'Old Nort really packed a shitty when someone let his cows out again.'

pack in Convey provisions into isolated area by horse or backpack.

pack of bludgers/drongos/no-hopers/prunes, etc Unimpressive group; eg 'Look at those jokers all wearing floppy hats. What a pack of prunes!'

packie The person controlling pack-animals.

pack it/shit 1. Nervous if not terrified

to the point of soiling your pants. 2. Talk nonsense.

packet from Paris A baby, probably arriving by stork.

paddle pop An iceblock, 60s teenage rhyming slang.

paddy batch Great batch of scones, after an Aussie rugby league player; also the nickname of recent New Zealand star batsman Mark Greatbatch.

pai/pie on Good or right; eg 'That new stretch of fencing is pai on.' Maori 'pai', good, 'pai ana', suitable.

pain in the puku Irritating person. Maori 'puku', stomach.

pair Breasts; eg 'What a pair on that sheila!'

Paka-Asia Pakuranga, an Auckland suburb recently enjoying an increase in Asian residents. Quoted in local *Evening Standard*, 8 November 1995.

94

pakapoo ticket, look like a/marked like a Confusing or incomprehensible, after the Chinese lottery ticket whose puzzling hieroglyphics to Europeans did not stop them participating in this illegal Housie type of gambling earlier this century.

Pakeha A non-Maori New Zealander. A Maori word of indeterminate origin.

Pakehatanga The culture of non-Maori or Pakeha New Zealanders.

paki/pakihi Bald patch on a man's head, from Maori word 'pakihi', a bush clearing.

Palmie Palmerston North.

Panama Road boys Rugby league lads from a strong league area, Otahuhu; Panama Road is adjacent to the Auckland suburb, in Mt Wellington. Rugby league commentator Graham Lowe has at different times identified the Iro and Ropati brothers as Panama Road boys.

pannikin boss Foreman, originally sheep station manager.

paper-collared swell White collar worker.

Parnell shout Paying for oneself, after an Auckland inner suburb.

Parrie Paremoremo prison.

pash/pash up Vigorous kissing and cuddling, with the passion not extending to sexual intercourse.

passion-busters Unromantic knickers, originally issued to female members of the Second New Zealand Expeditionary Force during WWII; the term is generally used for any undergarments considered an unreasonable barrier to male lust.

patch Gang insignia sewn onto jacket.

patsy Half-gallon jar of beer; from Patsy Riggir, queen of the local country music scene, whose surname sounds like the rigger or squarerigger, another name for the half-gallon jar.

Patu Squad 1981 anti-Springbok Tour protesters awarded themselves this nameplay on the Red Squad, who were in their view the more notorious of two squads of several hundred police created for crowd control, issued with the then new long batons, riot shields and helmets. The Patu Squad issued themselves with motorcycle helmets and the shields of righteousness.

pav Pavlova cake.

pavlova Snow; so identified by Jim Hickey, TV1 weather, 2 October 1989.

pavs and savs Pavlova and saveloys, traditional party fodder.

pay through the nose Excessive charge; eg 'If you want one of the new top-of-the-range BMWs, you pay through the nose.'

pea, pie and pud Piecart serving of mince pie with mashed potato and peas sloshed over with gravy.

peabrain Small of intellect; eg 'That peabrain never manages more than four-letter words in Scrabble.'

pea-shilling touche Silly way of saying 'two-shilling piece', obsolete version of 'centy went toin'.

pearler/purler Excellent person or thing.

pelt back To be beaten; teenage Kiwi slang variant on Australian meaning to be thrown from a horse.

Pennydivers Nickname for Maori Battalion.

pepperpotting Past policy of placing Maori families among Europeans in new housing projects.

Perfume Point North end of Cheltenham Beach, North Shore, Auckland, and many other places in New Zealand where the smell of sewage spoils the scene.

perve Lustful staring.

peter 1. Cash register, for which one unlikely explanation is that it was often netted by thieves, and Simon Peter was a famous net-man or fisherman.
2. Flagon of beer, for which a slightly less tenuous origin is the abbreviation of 'Peter-see-me', a Spanish wine named after Cardinal Peter Ximenes.

peter school Gambling den, probably from a loaded dice known as a 'peter', or a whist call of that name.

physio Physiotherapist.

pickle me knob! Dated exclamation, where 'knob' means penis; eg 'Gawd pickle me knob, I never thought he'd drain a yard of piss in one go.'

pickle me daisies! Dated exclamation of doubt; eg 'You reckon New Zealand can be the world's best cricketing nation in five years. Pickle me daisies!'

pickled eels' toenails and jujubes Answer to a littlie wanting to know what is for dinner.

picnic A problem. You may be intending to picnic on an island but if the weather turns nasty on the yacht there, you could be in a picnic.

piecart Caravan with hinged side-door through which fastfoods are dispensed. Often located near a railway station or bus terminus.

pig Flagon of beer.

Pig Islander New Zealander, from the land Captain Cook peopled with pigs.

pig out To eat excessively.

pigeon's milk Good liquor; eg 'Orrhh, fine drop of pigeon's milk, me old china.'

Piggy Nickname for Prime Minister Robert Muldoon, coined by Steve Whitehouse in a mid-60s student revue at Victoria University of Wellington.

pig's arse/bum/ear Exclamation of doubt and derision.

pig's poop and treacle Less crude response to the dinner question.

pigshit, treacle and fried worms Another answer to the dinner query.

pikau Backpack or swag, from Maori for a load on the back, or act of carrying it. This homemade item was often constructed from a sugarsack, small potatoes or rocks placed in the bottom corners, tied with rope to the corners and the top of the bag, securing the bag and forming shoulder straps.

piker Somebody who opts out of an activity, usually a drinking bout; eg 'Mike proved a piker again, never even came to the party.' Piking on your mates disappoints them, because you have not arrived. **Pike out on** your mates is to depart, perhaps in the sense of being rendered unconscious by excessive booze intake.

pikkie A picture, a photograph. The plural 'pikkies' is the cinema.

pill Rugby ball.

pimp Tell-tale.

ping Penalise, usually a referee decision in rugby, popularised by commentator Earle Kirton from 1989.

ping off Release a missile, usually a stone, from a shanghai or a beebee gun or something more lethal; eg from Glenn Johnston: 'We went out the bush and pinged off a few bunnies.' Word may derive from the sound, what Partridge calls an echoic coinage.

pinko A Communist or person of extreme left-wing political commitment, from the colour associated with Communism.

piss Alcohol, usually beer. A drinking session is **on the piss**, and you can **go on the piss** or **go out on the piss**.

piss all over Defeat easily.

piss awful Unpleasant.

piss easy Exceptionally easy to achieve.

piss in Act of easily achieving. In the Super Twelve final the Blues pissed in.

piss in someone's pocket Ingratiate yourself.

piss in the hand Something that is easily achieved.

piss in the wind Not easy and not recommended.

piss on regardless Determined drinking, ignoring consequences.

piss up large Drink long and hard.

piss weak Inadequate.

pissfart Insignificant person or fiddling around; eg 'How about we stop pissfarting about and finish this drain.'

pisshead Persistently heavy drinker.

piss on someone from a great height Give someone a very hard time; eg

'That bastard who conned all those pensioners out of their savings deserves to be pissed on from a great height.'

pissed as ten pigeons under a mock-amock tree Very inebriated, as pigeons become from feasting off the wineberry bush, and were easy pickings for Maori hunters; they were also about the closest pre-Pakeha Maori got to alcohol.

pissed out of your brain Totally intoxicated.

pissed to the eyeballs Full of booze.

pisser The pub.

pissing it up against the wall Wasting your money or resources.

pissing razorblades Painful urination, from an infection.

pissy-eyed Drunk.

place where the big nobs hang out Men's toilet.

placer A lamb whose mother has died and it has adopted a stone, bush or other object as a mother substitute.

plain as a pikelet Unprepossessing appearance; eg 'That new actor in *Shortland Street* is as plain as a pikelet.'

plastic fantastic Revolutionary all-plastic hull designed by Bruce Farr for the yacht KZ7 in the Kiwi challenge for the 1987 America's Cup. Also used of credit cards.

play the field Go after all possibilities, often in sexual sense; eg 'Tom enjoys playing the field too much to ever settle down to marriage.'

plonk Any alcohol, usually cheap and nasty. Originally a dire port sold by the quart.

plonker An idiot.

plum jam A lamb, in the rhyming way of shearers.

plunk a baby Give birth, a tribute to the Plunket Society's dedication to all Kiwi newcomers. Variations are **to get plunked**, **get trubied** after Plunket founder Sir Truby King, and **get karitanied** after the founding place of the society outside Dunedin. **To be plunked** is to be pregnant.

pluty Well off and/or assuming superiority over the rest of us ordinary Kiwi jokers. The plutocracy are found still in suburbs such as Fendalton, Remuera and Kelburn.

pogger To meander. 'An interesting perambulation with no rhyme or reason,' according to city council town planning officer Marilyn Ager quoted by Jack Leigh in his booklet *Exploring Auckland on Foot*, 1977.

poke a stick at, more than you can Supply exceeding demand. Too much of anything, like cricket or rugby at the end of the long seasons.

poke in the eye with a burnt stick, better than a One way of suggesting gratitude for something that is perhaps less than wonderful, but better than nothing.

poked Tired; eg 'I've been on a yacht in Cook Strait all day and I am utterly poked.'

pole To steal.

pollie A politician.

Polly Polynesian

Pom/Pomeranian/Pommie A person from Britain. May have developed last century from children rhyming 'immigrant' with 'pomegranate'.

pomcholygaflasma Amazing! As indeed is this nonsense word.

pong Stink. Maori 'puhonga' means stinking.

Pongo/Pongolian British person, first so among WWI soldiers, probably from the British forage cap resembling that worn by the dog Pongo in a Punch and Judy show.

pony Small glass of beer.

poo palace Homosexual bar.

poo pusher Active male homosexual.

poofter A male homosexual.

poohpooh Rifle or big gun in WWI, probably from the Maori word 'pu', a gun.

poon A loner.

poorman's orange New Zealand grapefruit.

poozling Scavenging in derelict buildings for recyclable items.

pop A try or chance at something, when you give something a pop or have a fair pop at something.

popular as a shit at a nightmen's picnic Very unpopular, as it would be for the emptiers of human waste if confronted by such whilst picnicking.

POQ Piss off quick.

pork/porking To engage a woman in sexual intercourse.

pork chop at a synagogue, to feel like a Embarrassed or uneasy.

pork pie A bad bruise; eg 'You know, Hughie, in Otahuhu we call a pork pie a haematoma on the leg.' Graham Lowe to Hugh McGahan on *Aussie League on Two*, 19 March 1993.

pork sword The penis.

Porkalofa Aucklander.

Porklander New Zealander.

possie Hiding place and/or useful position, originally Gallipoli dugouts.

possum Dear; eg 'Hello, possum, how's tricks?' Barry Humphries popularised this usage through his alter egoine, Dame Edna Everage.

possum popper Professional possum trapper.

pot To position a child on a potty. If someone **puts your pot on** it could mean you are exposed in wrongdoing.

pot-stirrer Anti-establishment activist, like many a protest leader.

potato A Polynesian, brown on the outside, white within.

poultice A large sandwich using all available ingredients, like an American dagwood.

pound to a pinch of goatshit – and you hold the stakes in your mouth Confident bet, extending the English phrase 'pound to a pinch of shit'.

Pressbutton A Presbyterian.

pressie A present.

pricey Expensive.

pricker Angry, in the phrase **to get the pricker with**.

prickhead Mild term of abuse that can be affectionate.

Proddy dog Protestant.

puckeroo To ruin. Maori 'pakaru', broken.

pug of neatsfoot Cup of tea. The pug was the housekeeper's parlour in Pongolia, neat's foot is a pale yellow oil of similar shade to tea, made from cattle bones and used to dress leather.

Pukatawhino 'Buggered if I know.' You have to say it quick. Often a response to the question 'Where is

Waikikamukau?', another placename that can be slowed, to render 'Why kick a moocow?' The usual response to that was, 'Because it kicked me.' Keri Hulme offers her childhood variant: 'Wheatawhakaue?' Answer: 'Pukatawhainau!'

pull a swiftie Deceive with some clever or dishonest move.

pull finger Hurry up.

pull someone's tit Tease or make a fool of.

pull your head/neck in Mind your own business. 'Pull your woolly head in — the woodpeckers are flying low' was the advice to troops in Korea.

punch a Pom a day Catchphrase of a decade back, when there was advertising advice to drink a pint of milk a day or eat an extra egg. All three propositions have fallen by the wayside.

punch out To beat someone up.

punch out a dark one To defecate.

punch shit out of To beat up someone.

punch someone's lights out Beat somebody badly enough to render them unconscious or unable to see, the lights being the eyes; or the internal organs, perish the thought.

punga The penis.

punter A pickpocket's assistant with the job of distracting the target.

purge Alcohol.

push a turd uphill with a toothpick
Very hard work.

push shit uphill Hard work.

pussy-knitting Reflections in puddles,
the way wool can look after a kitten
has played with it.

pussy power Power of the female sex
to control men, with sex, from 'pussy'
meaning the female genitalia.

put a horn on a concrete post
Appreciation of a properly completed
task, everything being there, such as
a slap-up meal with all the trim-
mings.

put across a beauty Do something
smart.

put an iron on your shoulder In debt.

put away your John Banks Don't use
your cellphone here! Early 90s reference to then Minister of Police John
Banks accused of using his cellphone
on a flight.

put in Betray or simply propose. You
could put in a slacker with your boss,
or you could put him in for a raise.

put into broodmare's paddock Be
made pregnant.

put one on To punch.

put one over To deceive somebody.

put the shits up Frighten someone.

put up with Endure. Parents put up
with screaming babies.

put you crook Mislead.

put your kicking boots on Achieve
accuracy, from goal kicking in rugby.

py korry By God; allegedly pidgin
Maori.

QFRTB Quite full, ready to burst; that is, belly very full of beer.

Quaky Isles, the New Zealand, being earthquake-prone.

quarter acre, the cult of the New Zealand preference from pioneering times for every family to have a quarter acre to put their house on. Austin Mitchell satirised it in his 1972 book *The Half-Gallon Quarter-Acre Pavlova Paradise*.

quarter-loaf South Island version of a half-loaf of bread.

quarts Outdoor tea, from being made in a quart-sized billy.

Queen City Auckland, after its main street.

Queen Street bushie/farmer City dweller with a farm.

Queen Street from Christmas, doesn't know Confused or stupid.

queer Mentally unsound; eg 'He's a bit queer in the head, that new boy.'

queer as a quacking quail Very peculiar.

queerie Simpleton or homosexual.

quick quid Money readily acquired. There's no longer a quick quid to be made from kiwifruit. A 'quid' was a pound note from c1920 until a pound became two dollars in 1967, but the quid-ity lingered on.

quick smart At once, on the double; eg C'mon, lads, let's have the chairs stacked quick smart.

quickie A swift sexual experience; eg 'Feel like a quickie, tonight, dear?'

quid, not the full Mentally defective.

quids, for Desired above dollars; eg 'I wouldn't miss that new production of Carmen for quids.'

quince Wimpy, effeminate person. **To get on somebody's quince** is to annoy them.

quite a few A lot, actually; eg 'Had quite a few beers last night.'

quite nicely Pretty nigh perfect; eg 'That'll do quite nicely, girls, the table settings are fine.'

quizzy Overly inquisitive.

quoit Backside. To go for your quoits is to run fast.

Rabbit killer

rabbit A young woman; eg 'Joel's making a fool of himself, going out at his age with a rabbit.'

rabbiting Causing a rugby ball to be carried illegally across the try line by a second movement.

rabbit-killer A death blow to the back of the neck using the side of the hand karate-style.

rabid Angry. Sixties teen slang. A girl could be rabid about mislaying her frosted pink lipstick.

race off To seduce.

racehorse Thin cigarette you rolled yourself.

radical! Exclamation of mock horror. 'No knickers under his kilt. Radical!'

rad-les-sep-fem Radical lesbian separatist feminist, the creature that sweeps into establishment male nightmares like Brunnhilde and her Valkyries.

radio with pictures Television, from the man who introduced it into our community in the early 60s, Director-General of Broadcasting Gilbert Stringer.

Rafferty's rules No rules whatsoever, from a boxing reference to a rough house. Extends to lack of honour and restraint, particularly in politics. Rafferty's rules could be said to apply in the first MMP Parliament.

rag No good; juvenile 90s slang.

rage Wild time or wild party, which can be ragey or a rage up. A rager is a party animal or drug binger who likes to rage all night.

raincoat Condom. Its use sometimes compared to 'taking a shower with your raincoat on'.

raining harder than a cow pissing on a flat rock/raining like a drunken dog Teeming down, the way it was every day in January 1989 in Auckland.

raise my rent! Exclamation of surprise; eg 'Ben's won the double again. Well, raise my rent!'

rajah The erect penis.

ram it down your throat Something forced upon you; eg 'Old Foxie's always trying to ram Shakespeare down Form Four throats.'

ram it up your bum What can be done with something unwelcome; eg 'Old Foxie can take his Shakespeare and ram it up his own bum.'

randy as a bitch on heat/a bushed billygoat/a drover's dog Panting for sex.

Rangitoto Yankee Aucklander, implying brashness.

rapt Ecstatic or at least pleased. Short for 'enraptured'.

rare as rockinghorse shit Extremely uncommon.

rark Hoon around in a vehicle.

rash, all over someone like a Tiresomely attentive, often sexually.

rat factory/house Psychiatric hospital.

ratbag 1. Nasty, eccentric, unreliable, troublesome, uncouth or worthless person.
2. Engaging rogue or unconventional fellow.

ratbaggery Unacceptable or eccentric behaviour; eg 'Every afternoon he hogs the pool table. Typical of his ratbaggery.'

rate of knots, a Travelling fast.

rations Sexual entitlement, often used negatively in 'cutting your rations'.

ratshit Poor condition, from a hangover or in relation to food or machinery. If you **don't give a ratshit** you do not care at all.

ratstail Rotten weather.

Rattler, the Christchurch/Greymouth express of yore.

rattletrap Rundown vehicle; eg 'Can you credit this rattletrap getting a warrant?'

ratty 1. Silly or slightly eccentric.
2. Irritable, angry.

ratty on/over Romantically impressed with someone.

razoos Testicles; corruption of the Maori word 'raho', bringing new meaning to the old phrase about people not being worth a brass razoo, or farthing.

razz To jeer. Probably from giving somebody the raspberry.

razzy roostered Pleasantly surprised; eg 'The way young Cutler's got the farm up and running in just a few weeks, why, I'm razzy roostered!'

rearend loader Active male homosexual.

reck Rubbish. Like a car that proves to be an unreliable rust bucket.

red as a beetroot/lobster As embarrassed as you get.

red ned Cheap red wine, originally a potent muscatel here and in Sydney.

red sails in the sunset Menstruation, often a male lament at it interfering with sexual activity.

redgees/regges The regulation patches or decorations on leather or denim gear that is part of gang attire.

Rehab, the The loan WWII returned servicemen received from the Rehabilitation Department.

rellies Relatives.

remit Branch directive for consideration by central executive.

Remmers Remuera, an Auckland suburb.

retread Worker back from retirement.

rev up 1. Put life into something, such as a party or an alcoholic beverage; eg 'This punch needs a rev up. I'll get the vodka.'
2. To make somebody feel anxious.

Richard Cranium A silly person, an elaboration of 'dickhead'.

rig Shark. Ministry of Ag and Fish prefers the spotted dogfish/pioke/gummy shark/smooth hound. Mostly South Island name.

rigger Flagon of beer, from the days when a quart flagon of beer was called a squarerigger.

right Favourable, in matey phrases such as **she'll be right** and **I'll see you right**.

ring around that, put a A certainty, such as the name of Christian Cullen at fullback for the All Blacks in 1997.

ringbark To fart.

ringbolter Stowaway.

ringie 1. The fastest shearer in the shed.
2. The keeper of the ring or betting pool in the game of two-up, thus the banker who dispenses winnings.

ring-in A substitute, often in a sporting contest.

rip To annoy, as in the once popular phrase **wouldn't that rip your ration book**.

rip into Engage vigorously, the way Super Twelve forwards enter a scrum. Often fisticuffs, or a severe reprimand.

rip, shit and bust A vow to make a huge effort.

ripper! Exclamation of approval.

RITP Rip into the piss, which is an invitation to drink up.

Riverhead mould Riverhead Gold brand of tobacco, with reference to its alleged dampness.

Rob's Mob Supporters of late Prime Minister Rob Muldoon, perceived as ordinary blokes.

robber's dog, in like a Keen.

rock chopper Roman Catholic, perhaps from initials.

rock college Prison.

rock your socks off Something that will surprise or excite you, often what deejays promise the music will do for you.

rod-walloper Male masturbator.

Rogernomics The free market reforms of Finance Minister Roger Douglas in the mid to late 80s.

roll-your-own Cigarette rolled by hand.

rooster Person. Amiably meant, often qualified as 'old' or 'odd'.

rooster one day, feather duster the next The up and down of life, particularly for performers and politicians.

roostered Worn out, often sexually.

rooster's blood Red wine.

root Sex or the object thereof.

root, hog or die Pioneering vow to make every effort.

root more, eat more, drink more piss! Redneck chant derived from the 1981 police Red Squad, which has the acronym 'red' celebrated in the phrase.

root my boot! Exclamation of surprise.

rooted Exhausted from whatever.

root-faced Humourless.

rooter Sexual enthusiast.

rootrat Active heterosexual.

ropeable Extremely angry.

rort 1. A scam, like the dubious welfare claims the authorities are trying to stop.
2. Something exceptional, often a party.

rotary hoe Right oh.

Roto-Vegas Rotorua, it hopes.

Rottenrua Rotorua, from the pervading rotten-egg stink of sulphur.

rough To beat somebody up.

rough as a pig's breakfast Uncouth.

rough as bags Uncouth.

rough as guts Tough but admirable.

round the world for threepence Drinking methylated spirits.

rousie Rouseabout or shearing shed hand.

rousie's chewing gum Sheep dags, the muddy, excrement-coated wool which form around the sheep's hindquarters.

rubber guts Someone lacking intestinal fortitude. Originally the German naval shell from the Kiwi point of view in WW1.

rubbish To dismiss or scorn.

rubbity The pub, as in 'rubbity-dub' rhyming slang.

rubydazzler Something superb.

rugger bugger Rugby fan.

rumty Anything excellent.

run-around, the Being misled.

run around like a blue-arsed fly/a chook with its head cut off Erratic behaviour, often manic, like a blowie buzzing a dead sheep.

run like a hairy goat Move very slow or very fast.

run past Present something to be looked at for an assessment. Treasurer Winston Peters has many papers run past him by his staff.

rustbucket Decayed car.

ruth Vomit, often in the phrase 'to cry ruth'.

Ruthanasia Policy of savage cutting back of state benefits by Minister of Finance Ruth Richardson, specifically her bill to reduce welfare benefits by $780 million from 1 April 1991, reported in *Time* magazine, 22 April 1991.

Ruth's Rottweilers Treasury officials keen to do her slash policy on state benefits. 'Ruth's rottweilers must not be allowed to dictate terms to the ultimate disadvantage of all.' Dr Ian Shearer, dean of Auckland Technology Institute, the *Dominion*, 20 June 1991.

S

Sailer

sailer Loose branch, one that will sail in the next high wind.

sale To vomit; usually you **make a sale.**

salmon day, a A work day wasted swimming against the current of problems and getting nowhere.

salubrious Fine weather among trampers, for whom salubing is sunbathing, a salubrium a rest in the sun.

salvage To steal or scrounge, originally WWI soldiers.

same as your tongue and a little older than your teeth My age is none of your business.

Sami Samoan. Originally prison term.

sammie Sandwich.

sandwich short of a picnic Mentally disadvantaged.

Sandy Hookers Nelsonians, specifically local musterers, from living near Farewell Spit.

s'arvo This afternoon, as in 'See ya s'arvo.'

save a match and buy a farm Adage encouraging thrift.

save it Keep it to yourself, I don't want to know.

save your money and buy a pie Decline of loan on grounds you need it more yourself.

saw and say nothing Hold your counsel. From sawmilling.

saw off me legs and call me tripod! Exclamation of surprise.

sawdust sandwiches Hard rugby practice indoors, usually in a sawdust-floored gym. Coach Frank Walker explained Wellington's win over North Harbour in the *Evening Post* of

14 August 1995 thus: 'I think it's those sawdust sandwiches they eat.'

sawing wood Snoring.

sawyer Weta, c1880.

scale/scale off To make a quick or furtive exit, or to catch an illegal tram, train or bus ride, possibly from the scale or weigh in of a jockey. Also extended to mean theft.

scaler Thief, especially from his mates.

scaly bloke Thin man, from 30s Depression.

scarce as hen's teeth In zero supply.

scarfies Dunedin students, from the scarves they wear at rugby games.

Scarfyville Dunedin. 'It meant putting in a few nights without booze in Scarfyville.' Marc Ellis, *Evening Post*, 8 March 1993.

schlong Penis, perhaps pretend Yiddish.

scody/scady Something admirable or not admirable. Street slang, deriving from skateboarding.

scone 1. Head.
2. To hit somebody on the head.
Do your scone is to lose your temper.
Off your scone means you are mad.
Suck your scone in is advice to stop talking nonsense or mind your own business. **Use your scone** is advice to act sensibly.

scone dough isn't properly mixed Dim-witted.

scone hot Superb. Last year Daniel Vettori was a scone hot cricketer.

scone in the oven Pregnant; variant of the bun therein.

sconegrabber A toddler.

scoot Drunken bout, usually in **on the scoot.**

Scotch mist and duck under the table Answer to 'What's for tea, Mum?'

Scotsman's grandstand Non-paying view of a sporting event.

scratch cat Woman of ill temper.

scratchie Lottery ticket from which you have to erase the covering to reveal the potential prize.

screwy Crazy, as you are said to be with a screw loose.

scroggin The dried fruit, nuts and chocolate that provide high energy and low burden in the bush, maybe from the dialect word 'scrog', a stunted bush.

scrousher Old digger down on his luck, fallout from the goldmining era.

scrub To reject, as a player might be scrubbed from the All Blacks.

scrummy Lousy, in the WWI Kiwi ranks.

scull/skull Drink alcohol enthusiastically, perhaps linked to the way a sculler moves water, more likely a variation on the Scandinavian toast 'skol'.

scunge To beg or borrow for keeps, as with cigarettes.

scungy Dirty person or place, such as a student flat.

seagull Casual wharf labourer.

seagull's breakfast Traditional bushman's breakfast of a yawn, a piss, a look around, with the addition of a walk on the beach.

section Plot of land to build on that has been getting smaller as its cost rises.

see a star about a twinkle Need to urinate.

see you in the soup, bring your own spoon Warning of hard times coming and expect to look after yourself.

seed beast Compulsive male masturbator.

seedless raisins Married man with no children, of army origin.

seen better heads on a glass of beer Not an attractive person.

seen better legs on a billiard table Thickset and unshapely legs.

seen more pricks than a dartboard Promiscuous person.

segg Luncheon sausage; originally

steak and egg sausage.

semi 1. Articulated vehicle, which is semi-detached.
2. The semi-final of sporting competition. Often in the plural form 'semis', because there are two by definition.

send up gutless Make fun of.

septic Any person or thing regarded poorly, like a Yank and a bank and a wank, and whatever else rhymes with septic tank.

serve, a A foul blow in rugby; often cited by commentators in rugby league matches. Possibly combining the innocent serve of tennis and the innocent work of a waiter in an ironic fashion, for the phrase is often presented as 'serving up'.

sesqui, a An incompetent mess, muddle or failure. From Wellington City Council's sesquicentennial celebrations in 1990, marking 150 years of Pakeha settlement in New Zealand with millions misspent on entertainment that pleased virtually nobody.

session A period of drinking alcohol.

set in a crack To resolve something quickly or be well placed. From late last century, when whips were in skilful use. Like somebody who held on to his Brierley shares through the crash and is now set in a crack.

set like a jelly Well placed.

sexo Randy person.

shackledragger An Australian, from

111

the shackles worn by early convict residents.

shagger's back Sore back from excessive shagging or sexual intercourse.

shagging wagon Van or station wagon where shagging is conducted.

shagnasty Salutation or greeting, as in 'G'day, shagnasty, how's it goin?'

shake your shirt Applying yourself, as when a labourer removes his shirt.

shakedown Temporary bed.

shaking hands with the wife's best friend Urinating male.

Shaky Isles, the New Zealand, land of earthquakes.

shangie Catapult, short for shanghai.

shanty A pub, from the goldfield days of tent hotels.

shark biscuit Boogie board.

shark 'n' shavings/taties Fish and chips.

shat/shat off Angry or depressed. Even the most casual observers of Parliament would have observed how one frontbencher was shat off by Labour jibes. Every time he has risen to respond, he has just about shat himself with rage.

she A substitute for 'it' in popular phrases such as **she'll be right/she's jake/she's apples/she's sweet**, all assurances that everything is fine.

she wouldn't know the postie was up her unless he blew his whistle A stupid woman.

sheepo Shepherd.

Sheffield blight The elimination of vegetation by axe or slasher, from the fine steel of Sheffield.

sheila Woman.

shellacking Severe beating, verbal or physical, on the field or down the back alley.

shellshock bread Poor quality bread to WWI Kiwi soldiers.

shepherding Deliberate interference with players who could apprehend the ball-carrier in rugby. Originally referred to a digger who had become a squatter and was aiming to keep others off the land he claimed.

she's all wool and a yard wide Fat woman.

she's had more pricks than a dartboard/pin cushion A promiscuous woman.

she's on 1. A woman regarded by male as available for sex.
2. Anything that is going to happen, such as a bet or a game; eg 'Reckon she's on for tomorrow if the weather holds.'

she's two axe-handles across Wide woman.

shick/shicker/shickered/on the shicker Drunk. From the Yiddish word 'shiker', to be drunk.

Shicker Express, the The first tram back after six o'clock pub closing pre-1967.

shimmy Singlet. From chemise, maybe.

shingle short Mentally challenged.

ship girl Prostitute working the ships.

shirtlifter Homosexual, possibly back to convict days, when a shirt was the only clothes issue.

shit a brick/shit a brick and fart a crowbar! Extreme exclamation.

shit a brick and build a house Exclamation, often at unexpected good luck; eg 'After five games when the left winger hardly touched the ball, shit a brick and build a house, he's in for three tries in the first half.'

shit all over Beat easily; eg 'In recent years the Auckland rugby union team has shat all over the opposition.'

shit bricks Be angry; eg 'Martin's shitting bricks about being dropped from the upcoming tour.'

shit, eh? Expression of ironic astonishment; eg 'Cullen's in the All Blacks. Shit, eh?'

shit-features Ugly person.

shit for brains Stupid person; eg 'When it comes to any eye-hand co-ordination, Monty's got shit for brains.'

shit in Win easily; eg 'Wellington will shit in against Wairarapa Bush.'

shit in your own nest Ruin or do something to your own disadvantage; eg 'Sacking half his Cabinet is just shitting in his own nest.'

shit of a thing Something unacceptable or unpleasant; eg 'Shit of a thing losing three quick wickets in the ten minutes before lunch.'

shit oh dear/oh dearie oh Exclamation of regret, if not lamentation; eg 'Bowled for a duck first ball in both innings – shit oh dearie oh.'

shit on the liver Ill-tempered; eg 'That politician's just shy really, but the way he always snaps in public, you'd think he had shit on the liver.'

shit oneself/one's pants Disconcerted by fear or anger; eg 'I was pulled up at the lights when all these dirty big evil bloody bikies surrounded me. Thought I'd shit meself.'

shit out of Missing something, maybe luck; eg 'Bowled by a rank full toss on 99. Poor Stephen was shit out of.'

shit someone off Annoy someone; eg 'He really shat me off coming round and banging on the door at two am, for no good reason.'

shit-puncher/stabber/stirrer Aggressive male homosexual.

shit sandwich Male homosexual act.

shit show, not a No chance.

shit tacks Afraid; eg 'When that rottie came at me, man, I was about to shit tacks.'

shithead Objectionable person.

shithouse Lousy condition.

shitty A really vile mood. Displaying such can be to crack/pack/throw a shitty.

shivers! Mild exclamation.

shoddy dropper Seller of cheap serge, c1932. Baker says it was our own underworld slang, used by the Australians later.

shook on Attracted to someone.

shoot off/through Depart hastily.

shoot your bolt Male sexual ejaculation.

shooting bunnies Farting.

short arms and long pockets Mean person.

short fuse/wick Quick tempered.

short of a sheet of bark/short of a shilling/shingle Mentally deficient.

short of change Mentally limited.

shot full of holes Drunk. WWI soldiers.

shot to the eyeballs Very drunk.

shotty Shotgun.

shouse Lavatory, diminutive of 'shithouse'.

shout Round of drinks, or a treat.

shovel it! Expression of disgust or disbelief, suggesting what you can do with your bullshit.

show A house. Frank S. Anthony writes in *Me and Gus* that they 'live in one show'.

show a point to To swindle, from late C19th.

shower, I didn't come down in the last Rejection of ignorance or gullibility. Indignant claim to know more than one is credited with.

shrapnel Small change. WWI soldiers referred thus to French currency, full of holes as if hit by shrapnel.

shrewdie Clever person or clever behaviour, often in the phrase **to pull a shrewdie**.

shrimp Small and/or wimpy person.

shufti A look. WWII soldiers from an Arabic word.

shunt Dismissal. Many civil servants got the shunt during government restructuring.

shut the gate Indicative of an unassailable situation, usually a team with an unbeatable lead. 'When the Blues passed 50 with ten minutes to go and Natal had only 3 points on the board, it was shut the gate.'

shut your neck! Be quiet!

shypoo Inferior liquor, or inferior anything. Possibly from Cantonese 'sai po', a little shop, probably imported by Chinese to goldfields, where a shypoo shanty was a sly-grog premises.

sickie A day off work allegedly sick.

sifting Taking it easy; eg 'It's great sifting around at the bach weekends, get the damned city out of your veins.'

silly as a two bob watch/wet hen Very silly indeed.

Silver Ferns National Kiwi netball team, after insignia worn on uniform.

sink Imbibe alcohol. Footy teams have been known to sink a few beers after a game.

sink the boot in To kick opponents, too common in games of rugby. Can be used metaphorically, as a politician might do verbally (as well as physically!) to an opponent.

sink the sausage/saussy/sav Intromit the penis.

siphon the python Male urination.

sit down and I'll feed you tomorrow Be quiet and patient.

sit on one's arse Being lazy.

sit up like Jacky Behave well or confidently, like an organ grinder's monkey, which was often called Jacky.

six o'clock swill Intense male drinking before the six o'clock closing time of pubs until 1967.

sixpence worth of God help me waiting at the chemist's door for relief Somebody looking seedy and in need of a tonic.

sixtynine! Shearers' warning of ladies approaching and the swearing to stop.

skate Disappear, in the phrase **do a skate**.

skate, go for a 1. Get into trouble. 2. Take a fall, literally.

skate around/over Evasive behaviour. Politicians are often accused of skating around the facts.

skerrick, not a Not even the smallest amount. From a Yorkshire dialect word for a small fragment. 'Can't help you, mate. I haven't a skerrick on me.'

skin a rabbit Undressing a child.

skinner Empty or broke. If the pub has no beer it's a skinner.

skinnier than a gumdigger's dog Gaunt.

skite To boast, which a skiter does when he is being skitey or boastful.

skizziest The best, in 60s teenage slang.

slabby Timber worker, from handling slabs of timber.

slackarse Lazy or tired.

slant/slant-eye/slit-eye Oriental.

slanter/slinter A trick, often a mean one, often in the phrase 'to work a slinter'.

slap on the wrist with a wet bus ticket, a Light punishment that scarcely fits the offence. Jim Anderton used this phrase in May 1997 about the Parliamentary Privileges Committee over its decision in regard to an alleged assault on John Banks by Winston Peters. Often preceded by 'better than ...' to indicate sardonic appreciation that whatever you got is better than nothing.

sleep in the ditch Kiwi soldiers' name for slivowitz, the potent plum brandy the locals plied them with during their early 90s peacekeeping role in Bosnia.

sleep in the dogbox/under the house In disgrace, usually of a domestic kind, like coming home drunk and threatened with such treatment, or the threat implied.

sleep in the star hotel/starlight hotel/star and moon hotel Open-air sleep, which tramps are often required to do.

sleep with Mrs Green Another open-air sleep.

sleever Drinking straw.

slipper Boot, and a euphemism for putting the boot in; eg 'A pity to see the Cardiff team captain put the slipper in.' Keith Quinn, All Blacks versus Cardiff at Cardiff Arms Park, 15 October 1989.

slop back Guzzle booze, c1925.

slops Beer.

slug Charge exorbitantly.

slumgullions and barmolic Evocatively nonsensical response to the question what is for tea?

slutdust The dust that is swept under the carpet or bed instead of removed.

sly grog Illicit liquor.

slyballs Dismissive term for a male.

smacked bottoms on toast A threat to a rowdy kid.

smacker The mouth.

smack-up A fight, c1906.

smart arse Obnoxious fellow, not at all clever, who may smartarse around.

smarty Impertinent person, usually a child.

smell, hang around like a bad Lurking nuisance who is unaware when his or her company not wanted.

smell like something crawled up your arse and died there You stink.

smell like the back end of a brewery horse Very smelly.

smeller Objectionable person.

smoke To leave. To **go into smoke** is to go into hiding, where you are **in smoke**.

smoko Refreshment break for workers.

smoothiechops/smoothieboots Ladies' man.

smoothiepuss Pretty woman.

smooze To kiss and cuddle.

snag Sausage. **A few snags short of a barbie** is somebody not all there in the brain department.

snaky Bad-tempered.

snap-and-snarl The wife.

snare To seize, as one might snare a snag.

snarf To gobble up food.

snarked off To be upset.

snarler Sausage.

snelt Sneak-thief, or a term of abuse.

snigged home To be wrapped up or pulled into place. From logging term 'snig', to drag a log.

snitcher Excellent person or thing. However, to **get a snitch on** is to take a dislike, from the opposite meaning of a snitch as someone who informs against you.

snodger Excellent person or thing.

snork Baby.

snufflebuster Spoilsport or wowser, one who works to rid the world of snuffy, or being drunk.

so poor a rabbit would have to take a cut lunch Rural South Island saying about impoverished farmland.

so tight he/she couldn't pass caraway seeds Mean with money.

so tight he/she wouldn't sell you the steam off his/her shit Memorably mean with money.

so tight you couldn't pound a tooth-pick up her/his arse with a pile-driver Astonishingly mean with money.

so tight you couldn't screw anything out of her/him with a post-hole borer up her/his bum Appallingly mean with money.

SOE Sold Off Everything, more usually called State Owned Enterprise, observed on a wall of the inner Wellington suburb of Brooklyn, 10 August 1990.

sook/sookie A wimp or a crybaby, as weak as the calf it originally referred to.

sool Set a dog on somebody, from the dialect word 'sowl', to handle vigorously.

sooner A nervy horse that is too eager.

sore toe, done up like a Over made-up or overdressed.

soss/sossy Sausage or penis.

SOTW Start of the weekend. Steve Parr, *Sale of the Century*, TV1, 1 September 1989.

sounds like a billygoat crapping in an empty kerosene tin A raspy voice.

sour grape Rape.

southerly buster Southerly storm, specifically the savage south wind that whips Wellington over several days about four times a year, infamous for wrecking the *Wahine* interisland ferry in 1968, referred to the previous century by Wellington writer Katherine Mansfield.

spanker Disc of dried cow dung used as a play missile by rural kids; eg 'We had fights with cow spankers. I'd love to have those days back climbing trees and throwing spankers.' Andrewina MacArthur on her Wellington childhood. Derives from cow-spanker, an Aussie dairy farmer.

spare me days! Long-suffering exclamation; eg 'God spare me days, do you have to keep making that racket!'

sparkie An electrician.

speaking into the big white telephone Vomiting into the loo.

spear tackle Driven by two opponents headfirst into the turf, a dangerous tackle.

spear the bearded clam Intromit the penis.

spew Emotional outburst, in phrase to have a spew.

spieler Gambler or con man. From German 'spieler', a player.

spit, the big Vomiting.

spit the dummy Display petulance or be defeated or in some way removed from an expected position. Paul Holmes on TV1 news break 8 June 1995 promoting an upcoming item about a politician resigning from his party said 'another National MP spits the dummy'.

splash the boots Urination by a male and expected fallout.

sponger Someone who takes but does not give, a bludger.

spoon A fool.

spot 1. One hundred dollar bill. 2. To pick the best land.

spotty 1. A fish. 2. A spotlight, often used to fish for flounder.

spreader A blanket; used by whalers here before it was recorded elsewhere.

spruiker A loud speaker, extolling entertainment or just sounding off. Possibly from Dutch 'spreken', to speak.

spud Pregnant; corruption of Maori 'hapu'.

spud-barber Fellow who gets to peel the potatoes in the army, WWI.

spunk Sexy-looking person, who is said to be 'spunky'. From word for semen.

Square Dinks, the First Battalion, New Zealand Rifle Brigade, WWI. From the shoulder flashes.

squarerigger The square gin half-gallon bottles adapted later for beer.

squattocracy Wealthy sheep farmers who assumed aristocratic status.

squeaker A child.

squeal like a stuck pig Shrill moaning.

squib A failure, from a damp squib.

squiz A look.

stand around like a stale bottle of piss Idle and maybe mopey.

stand out/stick out like a country shithouse/tits on a bull Obvious or conspicuous.

starter Ready to give something a try; eg I'll be a starter for this bungy-jumping caper.

starve/stiffen/stone the crows! Exclamation of surprise.

staunch Loyal, as gang members are to the death.

stayer 1. Someone who endures, usually in a drinking group, maintaining good mateship and liquor control. 2. A racehorse sure to last the distance.

steal the show Unexpected star turn, like Christian Cullen in the Hong Kong Sevens tournament.

steelie A steel ball-bearing used unfairly in the game of marbles, shattering glass and clay opponents.

steinie A small bottle of Steinlager brand beer.

stewed bugs and onions Another response to the question what is cooking?

stick Mate; eg 'G'day, stick, 'ow's it goin' then?' May be a contraction of 'stickman'.

stick it up your arse/gunga, etc Dismissive remark.

stick like snot to a wall Loyal.

stick to your ribs Hearty meal usually involving a lot of meat.

sticker Hunter's knife for sticking pigs.

stickman A well-performed heterosexual.

sticks, the 1. The provinces or remote rural area.
2. The rugby goalposts.

stick-up Delay.

stickybeak To snoop, or somebody who does so.

stiff Unlucky, but often meant ironically.

stiff cheese/cheddar Bad luck, old thing.

stiffy Erect penis.

stinker Hot, humid day.

stinkie Small clay marble, lowest in the marble pecking order, seen to stink in the sense of being inferior.

stipe Stipendiary steward, a race-course official.

stir Party; eg 'Great stir you had last night.'

stir the porridge Man having sex with a woman after another man.

stir the possum Cause trouble; eg 'Tank goes to every election meeting he can, just to stir the possum.'

stir the pot Cause trouble.

stirrer Troublemaker.

stocking Extortion, bullying, stand-over tactics by youth gangs on other children. 'Police said the gangs called it stocking.' The *Dominion*, 18 August 1992.

stoked Excited or drunk; eg 'Jim didn't expect to win in that field and he's stoked.'

stokers Those who stayed behind in the war and were suspected of keeping women's sexual fires stoked.

stonkered Exhausted, outwitted, defeated, drunk, in dire trouble. May derive from stonks, a game of marbles.

stop off To cease.

stoush A fight. In context it can be an appreciative reference to an outstanding, hard-fought rugby game, or a memorable fight in a game of rugby. From a dialect word 'stash' or 'studhie', a quarrel. In WWI artillery bombardment was referred to as 'The Big Stoush'.

straight off the turnips A country bumpkin.

straight wire, the The truth.

strain the potatoes Male urination.

streak A very thin person, often extended to **a streak of weasel piss**.

street cred Authenticity. Short for 'credibility' in a public situation, which often means teenage defiance of authority. Another youthful borrowing from the States.

strength of it, the The importance of something, or its reliability or extent.

stretcher case 1. Somebody crazy enough to warrant being stretchered off to a lunatic asylum.
2. Somebody playing a game regardless of a serious injury, or somebody who has just received a serious injury.

strike me handsome/lucky/pink Exclamation of surprise.

string along To deceive.

stripey Unconvincing, as in streaky.

stubbie Small bottle of beer.

stubbie short of a six-pack A bit dim.

stuck into Engage with gusto, as rugby forwards get stuck into each other. It can also mean to attack verbally or physically, which also often involves rugby forwards.

stuff To defeat comprehensively.

stuff, not give a To not care at all.

stuff and butter me! Exclamation of surprise.

stuff it up your jumper! Get lost! Do what you like.

stuff off! Go away.

stuff-up A major mistake.

stuffed Exhausted.

stumered Ruined, perhaps financially, for a stumer was a dud cheque. Often used in sporting or gambling contexts.

stunned Drunk.

sub A replacement player in a game of rugby.

subbie A sub-contractor.

suck off into the sunset! Go away.

suck the arse out of a durry Smoke a roll-your-own cigarette down to the last gasp.

suck-holer A toady.

suff Enough, as in 'sufficient'.

Sulphur City Rotorua.

sunburnt New Zealander A Maori.

Sunday dog Lazy mustering dog.

Sunday shearer Lazy shearer.

Super Twelve Rugby competition between 12 conglomerate provincial teams from South Africa, Australia and New Zealand.

superpompidious Excellent.

supersnagative First rate.

surf 'n' turf burger Fish and meat burger.

swag Backpack of the tramp or swagman/swaggie. To become one you **go on the swag**. If you have **a swag of** anything, you have a lot of it. If you are **looking for your swag straps** you are considering seeking another job.

Swamp Foxes Thames Valley rugby team.

swannie Bush shirt, from the brandname Swanndri.

swell Single woman earning lots of lolly, a female yuppie.

swept Cleaned out of money.

swerve, a Something you avoid. You might give a former girl-friend's invitation to her party a swerve.

swi/swy Two-up gambling, from German 'zwei', two.

swifty A trick, performed when you 'pull/work a swiftie'.

swipe Objectionable person, whom you might take a swipe at.

Taddie

TAB Totalisator Agency Board, state-appointed betting shop, beginning as off-course bookmaker on racehorses in 1949.

tabby Dotty old dame, supposedly because such dames surround themselves with cats.

tacker/wee tacker Child.

taddie tadpole.

taiho! Wait! eg 'Taiho a tick, will ya, Jean, I'm not quite ready.' A contraction of Maori word 'taihoa', which Williams translates as 'by and by'.

taiho the land court Advice to back off; local variant of the American phrase 'don't make a federal case out of it'.

taiho, touch your kick, your turn to cough up a quid It's your round of drinks; 'kick' was wallet, wherein was the required quid or pound note.

tailgunner Male homosexual.

tailor-made A cigarette that comes from a purchased packet, as opposed to one you roll yourself.

Takapuna surprise Steak stuffed with oysters.

take a long walk off a short plank Go away.

take out the back teeth Neutering the domestic tomcat.

take that and share it among you A pre-emptive remark from a belcher or farter.

take the bum off Change nappies.

take the burnt chops Work as a sheep musterer, from the tucker likely to be served such a worker.

take the day off to carry bricks A working holiday.

takey-ah-ways Takeaway food, pronounced as if it were Maori.

talk a glass eye to sleep Boring.

talk bullock Use bad language. Bullock drivers were known for it.

talk the leg off an iron pot Talk too much, and/or persuasively.

talking shit at the moon Talking rubbish.

talking to a brick wall Complaint that audience not paying attention.

tall poppy Outstanding person who has aroused the envy of lesser achievers. The phrase was coined in 1931 by New South Wales premier J.T. Lang to describe those on government salaries above 10 pounds a week. The **tall poppy syndrome** is used of a high-flier shot down by disapprovers.

tall timber Lofty line-out forwards in rugby union. All Black lock Gary Whetton observed tall timber in the Queensland side on TV1, 20 April 1991; winger Bernie Fraser spotted them among the Scots in their game against the All Blacks at Murrayfield, TV1, 21 November 1993; Stu Wilson saw them in the North Harbour versus France game on TV1, 12 June 1994.

Taranaki Contemptuous adjective, mostly in the South Island, earlier this century; eg 'Real Taranaki beast, that one, proper cow of a bull.' Taranaki has been singled out among Kiwi provinces to represent things excessively rural or in the hick category, but some of the following entries would rate at the other end of the scale.

Taranaki bullshit Boasting.

Taranaki cow Any poor cow condition-wise.

Taranaki gate Home-made gate.

Taranaki spanner Bottle opener.

Taranaki sunshine Rain.

Taranaki topdressing Cow dung.

Taranaki violin Cowbells.

Tas/Tassie The Tasman Sea.

tatt Tattoo.

teapot Hands on hips. 'Angus Fraser gave it the old teapot, hands on hips on his follow through,' Glenn Turner observed to fellow commentator Henry Blofeld of the fast-bowler pausing to teapot and glare at batsman Martin Crowe, who had just hit a boundary off him in the England versus New Zealand test match at Lancaster Park, 9 February 1991.

tear-arse Treacle or golden syrup, with reference to its laxative qualities; c1920.

tear into Attack, with fists, words or gusto; eg 'He tore into his chores like there was no tomorrow.'

tear up for arsepaper Severe reprimand; Kiwi army WWI.

technicolour yawn Vomit.

teeth like a row of condemned houses Decayed teeth.

teeth on him/her like a donkey eating

thistles The big, strong variety.

teev Television.

tegel pigeon Kereru or native pigeon, employing jokey use of a popular frozen chicken brandname.

ten bob to a green gooseberry/nob of goatshit A confident assertion from the days when a 'bob' was a shilling; eg 'Ten bob to a nob of goatshit the Blues win the final.'

TF Tomato flavouring, if you are being polite; tucker fucker, if you are not.

that didn't touch the sides The first or second beer on a hot day after hard yakker and the implied request for more of the same. Popularised by McPhail and Gadsby in the pub segment of their TVNZ comedy series.

that ripped the fork out of your nightie That surprised you.

that'll be the frosty Friday/frozen fortnight Indicative of doubt or rejection.

that'll steam your socks off That will surprise.

that's a bit hot/much Protest at something adjudged unreasonable.

that's borer dust Dismissing something as nonsense, probably a euphemism for 'bullshit'.

that's you pressed off and buttoned To spruce up someone or something.

the fuck Introductory intensive, often responding to a request or command; eg 'The fuck I'll take the dog walkies, that's your job.'

there goes the Ohakune nut Spotting a redhead, from Ohakune being carrot country.

there's corn in Egypt yet Response to receiving more change than you expected; extension of the English phrase 'corn in Egypt', plenty of food.

they're off, Mr Cutts The race has begun. Possibly derives from the Cutts brush hurdle at Riccarton Racecourse.

thick as pigshit Very dim-witted, often with the addition **and twice as smelly.**

thick piss up the front bum Male ejaculation into vagina.

thicker than maggots on an old ewe's bum Plentiful.

things you see when you don't have your gun Comment of resignation or regret, such as a randy man seeing a woman he cannot pursue.

Think Big Ambitious and expensive state projects of the Muldoon era of late-70s, early-80s that were perceived as not delivering, making the phrase bywords for rash investment.

think you're clever but your feet stink You might well fancy yourself, but we don't.

think your shit doesn't stink, but your

farts give you away Your ego trip is not shared by us.

thinks only of his belly and what hangs off it A man whose thoughts never stray from food, drink and sex, the implication that there are other, perhaps worthier things in life.

thinks with his dick A man preoccupied with sex.

thirsty, I'm so ... I could scull the cap/scab off a can of beer Urgently desirous of alcoholic refreshment.

three pennorth of God help us Worthless creature.

Three Wise Men The All Blacks selectors.

throw The value of something, used in conjunctive phrases such as 'ten cents a throw', from the cost of a sideshow turn.

thugby Rugby, to those who also regard it as a form of open-air wrestling or an excuse for a stoush.

tickets on yourself Conceited, as you would be if you purchased tickets on your own performance.

tickle To steal, used in phrase 'tickle the peter', to rob the till, from early 30s.

tiffin Midmorning smoko, possibly from the Anglo-Indian 'tiffin', a light lunch.

tight as a bull's/duck's/fish's/gnat's arse Mean with money. The most pop-ular 'duck's arse' carries the extension ... and that's water tight.

tight five, the The five forwards who bind the rugby union scrum, namely a hooker and two props in front, behind them two locks.

tiki-tour Unlicensed driving; eg 'When I was twelve I had an old BSA Bantam motorbike hidden on the farm, and used to tiki-tour all round the back of Cambridge.' *New Zealand Herald*, 22 February 1989. Also means to look around. Possibly derived from Contiki tourist operators.

tiku on a stick The answer to what's for tea?

tinny A can of beer.

tin arse/bum Lucky person.

tin can Old, noisy car.

tin-canning/tin-kettling Beating of noisy kitchen utensils on pots and pans to celebrate a wedding or other occasion.

tin of cocoa, tin of cocoa, tin of Coca-Cola Cod-Maori greeting from 'tena koutou, tena koutou, tena koutou katoa'. When invoked by Tom Scott in a satirical rendering of a speech by Governor-General Sir David Beattie, Sir David's response was to present Scott with a tin of cocoa.

tinpot Insignificant and/or run-down. After the government reforms of the 80s, many small towns looked tinpot.

tin-teller Money-dispensing machine.

tingle Telephone call; eg 'Give me a tingle when you're ready.'

tinned Chinamen C19th goldfields phrase for Chinese miners' corpses shipped home for burial.

tinny Lucky.

tired and emotional Drunk.

tired as a newt Drunk; variant of 'pissed as a newt'.

titoki Shandy that includes raspberry, which looks like juice of titoki berry.

tits in a tangle In difficulty; eg 'Don't get your tits in a tangle.' Russell Tulloch on *Heartland*, TV1, 11 July 1995. Refers to the problems associated with the clothes mangle attached to washing machines in the days before spin-drying.

ti-tree oneself Take shelter from artillery bombardment, WWI. Last century Maori were said to **go ti-tree** or 'go bush' when they concealed themselves from advancing troops.

tizzy up Dress up.

to and from A Pom, originally among prisoners of war under the Japanese, WWII.

toa Champion marble; from the Maori for a warrior.

toby The tap system controlling water supply to a property.

toe Power/speed ratio, which has been applied in the TV car ad 'more toe than an Aussie tank', and memorably by Arran Pene, former All Black Number Eight, commenting in coverage of the All Blacks against a Scottish Development XV on 17 November 1993: 'Eric Rush has **got more toe than a Roman sandal**.'

toerag/toeragger/toerigger Obnoxious person, from whalers' version of Maori term of contempt.

toey 1. Excitable, anxious, touchy. 2. Fast, usually of a car or sportsperson or animal.

toity The toilet. If something has gone **down the toity** it is lost or has failed, like the majority of Lotto tickets.

Tommy Dodd Small glass of beer, late C19th.

Tongan steroids Mashed taro. 'Taro gives Jonah his power,' said his mother Hepi Lomu in the *Evening Post*, 17 June 1995. 'We joke it's Tongan steroids.'

tonky/toney Fashionable, as in swanky and high-toned.

too much Weet-Bix Superior strength. You could say that in the Ironman race the winner had too much Weet-Bix for the others. It is not officially an ad for the breakfast cereal Weet-Bix.

tooted Grazing animal poisoned by the tutu plant.

top shelf The best, from where the

best quality goods and liquor are kept.

toss your lollies To vomit.

tote The TAB on the racecourse precincts.

tote up To add up.

touch Somebody's turn to buy a round of drinks.

touch of the tarbrush Somebody with Maori blood.

touch your kick Modest loan, when a kick was sixpence.

touchy Over-sensitive; eg 'Don't stare at the braces on her teeth, she's touchy about them.'

touchy-feely Wimpy behaviour. Management consultant version of encounter grouping, used by late Rob Muldoon to describe management consultant Michael Gourley after he was employed in early 1988 to improve relationships within the Labour caucus.

towie Tow-truck driver.

town bike A sexually available woman.

trap for young players, a A danger to the young, inexperienced or naive, like taking out too many mortgages.

trol Female, less offensive than 'trollop'.

Toyota Corroda Jokey reference to Japanese cars perceived as tending to rust, punning on the popular Toyota Corolla.

treaclearse Unlikeable or sycophantic, or both.

Triangle Dinks Third Battalion, New Zealand Rifle Brigade, WWI. From shoulder flashes.

trick An amusing child.

tripe, don't bust a Take it easy, you might pop a gut-string.

tripehound Sheepdog.

tripes out, I'll tear your A threat unlikely to be executed.

troppo Crazy. From WWII servicemen in the tropics, where they often went troppo.

trot A person, usually affectionate, curiously, considering it was once an English word for a whore.

trot, a good/a bad A situation where fortune smiles or frowns on you.

trot, on the In sequence.

trots 1. Diarrhoea.
2. Horse harness racing.

truck and trailer Sycophant.

true dinks Assurance of truth, a contraction of 'true dinkum'; eg 'True dinks, Mike, I never laid eyes on your bag of marbles.'

trump of the dump Person in charge,

originally army officer.

trunk-muncher Cunnilinguist.

tryondewondygong Thingummyjig.

tryontwentygobbler As you asked, that's what I'm cooking.

TTFN Ta ta for now, or goodbye.

tucker Food, originally goldminers' rations.

tucker fucker Army cook or tomato sauce.

tugger Twit or male masturbator.

tukus Male underpants. In the *Dominion* of 6 June 1997 Frank Haden wrote of hearing Lower Hutt schoolboys discussing birthday presents, one saying 'and I got some new tukus'. A reference to NZ First MP Tukuroirangi Morgan, who attracted much publicity by purchasing expensive underpants.

tulip muncher Dutch person.

turbo suckout A wave breaking hard and fast in shallow water.

turboburger Double hamburger with beetroot, mayonnaise, lettuce, cheese, pickle, onion, grated carrot, tomato sauce, mustard, all guaranteed to rev you up; speciality in downtown Whakatane hamburger joint.

turd bandit/burglar/puncher/tapper Active male homosexual.

turd strangler Plumber.

turkey will roost on your lip, a Warning to a sulking or pouting child.

turn it on Give a party or provide drinks.

turn it up Make oneself sexually available.

turn on the Waipori Switch on the electricity; from one of the Central Otago rivers dammed for electricity.

turn-out Gathering, something politicians hope to see plenty of at election time.

turps Alcohol, often in phrase **to get on the turps**. From turpentine.

tussock jumper Station hand.

tussocker Somebody arriving in time for tucker, but after work has ended.

tweeds Trousers.

twin-set and pearls set Ladies of upper middle conservative class, from the dress they wear.

twist the tail Kid or tease. Possibly from tailing, to drive or tend animals.

two bastards on bikes Reaction in game of two-up from those betting on two heads when two tails come up.

two bob each way Hedging your bets, acting indecisively.

two ladies on bikes The reaction from tails bettors when two heads come up.

two pages stuck together Bit deficient mentally.

two-pot screamer Somebody with a low tolerance for booze.

two-minute silence The *Hokitika Guardian*, or any other paper adjudged thin on content.

two sandwiches short of a picnic A bit dim.

two shakes of a dog's hind leg A short interval of time, often used to assure somebody you will not take long.

two thirds of five eighths of fuck all Very little, often used to indicate disgust.

two-up Illegal gambling game where two pennies are tossed and bet on coming down heads and tails or two of either. From late C19th in Australasia, usually around pubs. No longer common here, but booming in Australian casinos.

two kumaras short of a hangi Simple-minded.

two tin of cocoa, two tin of jam. Timaru! Oamaru! Hi! Nonsense chant sending up Maori greeting, seen performed in a light-hearted rugby match among golden oldies at Ruatahuna, on the *Heartland* series, TV1, 11 July 1995.

tyke Catholic. From 'Teague', Ulster name for a Roman Catholic, which is from English version of Irish 'Tadhg', an Irish person.

tyrekicker 1. Used-car salesman or a car-yard browser.
2. A politician who is evasive.

Up large

ugly enough to eat gorse Term of abuse that suggests a resemblance to those gorse-munchers, goats.

uglier than a cow facing south Rather ugly.

Uncle Tom Cobley and all Rubbish, in a roundabout fashion from the cobbler's last or awl being rhyming slang for balls.

under the affluence of inkahol, though some stinkle peep I am Self-condemned drunk.

underground mutton Rabbit.

unemployed, the The penis, during period of sexual hibernation.

uni University.

unit 1. Wellington suburban electric train.
2. A year's worth of university study of a subject, with nine units required to attain a Bachelor of Arts degree.

Unsmiling Giants, the All Blacks up to the mid-80s, when Auckland flair under coach John Hart spread upwards and outwards.

up and under A rugby ball punted high in the air to allow a team to descend on the unfortunate opposition at the same time as the ball.

up at Rosses having afternoon tea with a straw hat on Facetious answer to question where are you going?

up Cook's arse Expression of disgust.

up in Lizzie's room behind the clock The less-than-serious answer to a question where something might be found.

up large Heavy drinking, sometimes extended to 'piss up large'.

up Mully's gully shooting magpies with a goss knife The reply to the question where are you going?

up shit creek in leaky gumboots In trouble.

up sticks To pack your belongings and depart or abandon your home and move on.

up the boohai for the rhubarb season/shooting peanuts with a sling/shooting pipis with a hayrake/long-handled shovel/shooting pukakas/shooting pukakas with a pitchfork/ popgun/ shotgun Lost and maybe loony, but more usually some of the droll extensions of being 'up the boohai' as a dismissive answer to a pesky question about what you are doing or where you are going, which you do not want to answer.

up the chute Wrong and maybe stupid or worthless; eg 'Sorry, fella, you're up the chute if you think New Zealand's going to lose the next America's Cup.'

up the Cook's Exclamation of encouragement, probably linked to the nickname of a regiment.

up the duff Pregnant, perhaps by extension from being in the pudding club, which could also be a plum duff.

up the Dutch shit In deep trouble.

up the Mokau Very lost, as you would be up this remote North Taranaki river.

up the river in a matchbox shooting pipis with a popgun Another of those evasively extended answers to where you are going.

up the scrub In the bush.

up the wop 1. Pregnant.
2. Broken or malfunctioning, as often happens to battery-driven toys.

up with the play Alert to what is happening, usually in sport, as a player or a spectator; eg 'Telly's okay, but you have to be there to keep up with all aspects of the play.'

up you for the rhubarb season Mildly abusive rejection, indicating you are talking rubbish.

up your nose with a rubber hose Jokily abusive rejection, which can be topped with the response – **twice as far with a chocolate bar.**

useless as a gumdigger's dog/tit on a hand/tits on a bull Completely useless or incompetent.

user pays Bureaucratic euphemism for screwing more money out of the public from traditional public services, one of the pettier examples of market-driven restructuring of the public service.

ute Utility truck or van.

Vegemite

vag A vagrant. If you are 'on the vag' you are on the road and maybe seeking work.

vaginamite Sexually overactive heterosexual male.

Vandemonian Literally somebody from Tasmania or Van Diemen's Land, which used to mean a convict, or in New Zealand an escaped convict, and by association, somebody rough or aggressive, then latterly immigrants from Tasmania.

vegemite Cute word for a child, perceived as a consumer of the yeast spread Vegemite.

vegemite driller Active male homosexual.

vegetable Dazed. Used by streetkids to indicate a doped state brought on by substance abuse.

vegetable sheep A South Island plant resembling resting sheep.

vegies Vegetables.

verbal diarrhoea Running off at the mouth.

vertical drinking Stand-up drinking, the way it was.

very funny Not funny at all; eg 'You think letting down her tyres was a good joke? Very funny!'

violets growing out of your ears Too good to be true; eg 'The smarmy way that girl lisps and pouts makes me sick. She's got violets growing out of her ears.'

visual symphony, a Ironic admiration of something way over the top, as employed by Lyn of Tawa in relation to the extraordinarily kitsch set in her Mitre 10 TV ad.

Vitamin DB Draught bitter from Dominion Breweries.

Waiouru blonde

W

wacker/whacker 1. Male masturbator. 2. A stupid and/or nerdy person.

waddy A club.

Wadestown Wadical Any mild if not lapsed socialist, after the cosy yuppies who inhabit the wealthy Wellington hill suburb of Wadestown without feeling the need to be any more radical than joining the local Labour Party branch.

wahine Girlfriend or wife, from Maori for 'woman'.

Waikikamukau Imaginary archetype of Kiwi back country town, a cod-Maori construction. 'Wakikamukau?' children ask each other. 'Because it kicked me.'

Waiouru blonde A sheep handy to army training area.

Waiouru limp An injury sustained in pursuit of Waiouru blonde.

waipiro Alcohol, from Maori for 'stinking water'.

waiwai Beer or any booze, from the Maori for 'sodden', the end result of too much waiwai.

waka blonde Maori woman. The reference derives from 'Whakarewarewa wahines', the Rotorua Maori women observed by European tourists.

wake up to Aware of something, on your guard against being duped; eg Sooner or later she'll wake up to his tricks.

walk-up/walk-up fuck Promiscuous woman — you walk up and ask her.

walloper Male masturbator.

wally Short back and sides haircut, named after Auckland barber Wally Buck.

wallyburger with cheese, fries and a large Coke The ultimate 'wally' or idiot, an extension of the English 'wally', not of the barber above.

Wanganella weather Good weather, from that following the *Wanganella* striking Barrett Reef off Wellington in 1947, allowing the ship to be floated to safety a few hours before a savage southerly struck.

wants the penny and the bun too Greedy; from the days when a bun cost a penny.

warratah Fence post.

waterfront solicitor Wharf labourer, because he is always working on a case.

wayback A remote rural district.

Way Down Under New Zealand, the way Kiwi soldiers sung it in WWII: 'For we are the boys from way down under, sons of the Anzacs are we.'

weak as cat's/gnat's/nun's piss Feeble and unthreatening; eg 'Their line-out is as weak as cat's piss, we'll have no worries there.'

Weasels Workers Communist League, a Maoist left-wing student activist group that penetrated Wellington student and trade union structures in the 70s and 80s.

weekend root Casual sexual partner.

weights up, put your Getting someone into trouble, perhaps from the weights carried in handicapped horseraces.

weird and wonderful Anything unusual or interesting.

weka A Chatham Islander.

well gone 1. Deeply in love.

2. Severely wounded. WWI.

well, I'll go to the pictures! Exclamation of surprise; eg 'You say you won Lotto's fourth prize four times – well, I'll go to the pictures!'

well, saw off me penis and call me Venus! Surprise, surprise! No sexual connotation. You might say it if you came home from work and saw a neighbour who'd neglected his house for 20 years busy scraping the paint and putting on primer.

well, what do you know? Indicative of mild or mock surprise; eg 'Well, what do you know, Michael Jones has made the All Blacks.'

Wellingmonian Resident of the capital city.

welter, make a Go to extremes.

were you born in a tent? Sarcastic enquiry of somebody who has left a door open.

West Coast sidestep Straight ahead, Greg Clark advised in the third rugby league test between New Zealand and Great Britain, 6 November 1993.

Westie Inhabitant of a western suburb of Auckland.

wet area An area that has voted to allow sales of liquor, which is now the vast majority of the country, as formerly dry areas have gone wet.

wet bread and butter bowling Cricket tactic of using the old ball after 85 overs have elapsed and the new ball is available, so that the ball becomes spongy and trickles off the bat, making scoring runs difficult. Commentators Parker and Galloway discussed such bowling during Radio New Zealand coverage on 26 February 1989.

wetboot man Bureaucrat, one who can't keep his boots dry in the bush.

whale into Attack vigorously.

wharfie Wharf labourer.

what a spaz! Jeering exclamation, short for 'what a spastic'.

what are you going to make out of it? Belligerent challenge.

what can you say to a pig that grunts? Rhetorical question about somebody adjudged hopeless.

what did your last slave die of? Sarcastic exasperation implied in this question that someone like a child or spouse is lazy and should do whatever themselves.

what do you call a fish with a cellular phone? A guppie.

whatever blows your dress up Reassurance that you are entitled to your own choice, even if I maybe might question your taste.

what's crawling on you? Request to be told what is upsetting.

what's the butcher's name? Sarcastic response to an obvious question, such as 'Do you really like Cadbury's Roses chocolates?' The phrase spread from its orgination in Feilding, where the butcher's sign read: 'Watts' the Butcher's Name'.

when the tui sings, we'll be rich Hopeful saying of the Coromandel gumdiggers.

where do bulls go for their honeymoons? Tuakau.

where were you when they were handing out the brains? You dolt.

wherever you may be, let the wind blow free May good fortune, good health and good weather attend you.

whingeing Pom British immigrant complaining about life here.

whinger Persistent complainer.

whiny Somebody who complains, or the complaining sound of a voice, like a hungry cat.

whips of Plenty of whatever.

white lady Methylated spirits, which turns white in water.

white Maori 1. An obsolete phrase for a Maori who adopted Pakeha name and/or ways.
2. Tungstate of lime, a miners' phrase, also obsolete.

whitebait Skinny person. Glenn Johnston offers the example: 'He's built like a racing whitebait.'

whitebaiter Maori activist, who baits whites or Europeans.

white hairs, you must have Said of somebody receiving an unexpected favour.

white-haired boy A favourite.

who slapped Nelly in the belly with a wet flounder? She's pregnant.

whojamaflung/whojamafiffle Thingummyjig.

whole box and dice, the Everything involved. We've packed everything for a week in the bush, the whole box and dice.

whopcacker/wopcacker Outstanding person or thing, perhaps evolved from a 'wopper' or large lie.

who's milking the cow? Who is in charge here?

whoshanwallah, ya little luggergate! Go away, you little brat.

who's up who and who's paying? Enquiry about what is happening, but originally a WWII sexual joke.

why don't you go and raffle your doughnut? Go away. Could be construed as a rude request, where your doughnut is the back or front bum.

why's a duck? The faster it swims. Quacker. One way to confuse a child asking a question you don't want to answer. Could be an extension of the nonsensical Marx Brothers' question, 'Why a duck?'

widgie Female partner of a bodgie, dressed to outrage 50s sensibilities with short blonde hair and short dress and heavy make-up.

widow-maker Loose limb of a tree, which can kill a forestry worker.

wigwam for a goose's bridle Jokey answer to a query about what you are making. Sometimes with the elaboration ... **to wind up the sun on a wet day.**

Wild Cats and Tigers Union The New Zealand Women's Christian Temperance Union's jokey acronym.

wild Irishman Matagouri plant, its thorns making it difficult to handle.

wild Spaniard Speargrass, its leaves like a Spanish dagger.

Willie Away Rugby union tactic of peeling off the front of the line-out around the back of the other forwards and leading a surge upfield. Named after 1958-65 All Black captain Wilson Whineray and used as the title of his book.

wind blows up your trouser leg and waggles your tongue Windbag or boaster.

Winterless North, the Northland before 1988's Cyclone Bola.

wiwi A Frenchman, a Maori colloquialism from the French 'oui oui' or 'yes yes'.

wobbly A tantrum. Often used in the phrase 'chuck/throw a wobbly'.

woo A mild petting session.

wood on, have the Enjoy an advantage, from woodchopping competitions.

Woodbine British soldier to Anzac counterparts, from the cigarette brand.

woodchook Weka.

wooden To hit. To **wooden out** somebody is to knock them to the floor.

wooden aspro A truncheon.

woody A woodsman.

woofar Willing worker on organic farm, cited on TVNZ *Eyewitness News*, 2 May 1989.

woolbug Shearer.

wool king A big sheep owner.

Woollies' blackballs/Woolworths' blackballs Sheep dags.

woopknacker A rough diamond character.

wopwops Remote place. Often said to be **in the/out in the wopwops.**

working for the Prime Minister On the Welfare benefit; eg 'Some surfers in the north jokingly say they are working for the Prime Minister, which means they are receiving the benefit.' Acting Director-General of Social Welfare Robin Wilson, the *Dominion*, 24 May 1991.

worse than a man short Useless worker.

would be if he/she could be Talentless trier.

would shit anywhere Uncouth person.

would you rather walk a mile and climb a stile or eat a sunburned cake? Question addressed to somebody lagging behind, often a child.

wouldn't call the king me uncle Expression of high spirits, higher than being related to royalty.

wouldn't it! Expression of dissatisfaction, exasperation, disgust, often extended in such phrases as **wouldn't it make you spit/make you spit chips/rip your ration book/rock you/root you/rotate you/rotate your crops/rotate your socks.**

wouldn't know sheep dung from dried dates Dim, if not dense.

wouldn't know shit from clay – unless you tasted it Severely limited person.

wouldn't know someone from a bar of soap/if you fell over them Not known to the speaker.

wouldn't know the Pitt Street/Brooklyn/Brighton tram was up them till it rang the bell and people started getting off Mean or dim.

wouldn't know your arse from a hole in the ground/from your elbow Ignorant or dim-witted.

wouldn't lend you the harness on his/her nightmare Mean person.

wouldn't piss down someone's throat if they/their guts were on fire Held in contempt.

wouldn't say bum for sixpence/shit for a shilling A non-swearer.

wouldn't that rip the crutch/fork out of your nightie/undies? How annoying or disgusting.

wouldn't touch it with a red-hot poker Extreme distaste.

wouldn't use whoever for shark bait Contemptible whoever.

wouldn't want whoever farting in my last pound of flour Fat person who would be sure to spread flour explosively.

wouldn't work in an iron lung Lazy person.

wowser Spoilsport or puritan, objecting to alcohol, cigarettes and any other joys that it is possible to kill. Originally a prohibitionist. Possibly from dialect word 'wow', to whine, acronymically identified by John Norton as 'We Only Want Social Evils Remedied'.

wozzed Very tired.

wozzle Wireless.

wrap Praise. Often used in sport in the phrase **to give someone a wrap**.

wrung out like a dishcloth Exhausted.

WWW World Wide Wait. Computer-user frustration at the World Wide Web.

XXXX

XXXX 1. Pimply young man in a white shirt who deals with foreign money exchanges, also known as a forex dealer.
2. Dark brown Waikato beer, challenged by Queensland tinnies, whereas forex lads have in many cases faded without challenge.

XYZ The YMCA as an ironically upended acronym among WWI soldiers.

Y

yank tank

yabber Chatter.

yakker Work.

yammer To complain.

yank tank Any large American car.

ya-yas German tourists, from their habitual deferential use of 'ja', German for 'yes'.

yarra Silly person. If you're silly enough to ask what a yarra is, then it's because yarra useless.

yee-ha! Exclamation of exhilaration.

yodel over the mahogany Vomit in a bar or over the toilet seat.

you can beat an egg, but you can't beat a root Sexual boasting.

you can choose your friends, but you can't choose your rellies Relatives just have to be tolerated.

you can put a ring around that Something that you can be sure of.

you can say that again! Assurance of agreement.

you can't fatten thoroughbreds Classy people are thin, okay?

you can't put a cow-cover over a horse and expect to get milk in the morning You must be realistic.

you could cut the air with a knife A tense atmosphere.

you could eat your dinner off that floor A clean house.

you could knock me down with a feather Expression of surprise.

you could whip a cricket over it any time Impoverished land.

you couldn't kick a Chinaman off your sister You are pathetic and I'm a racist.

you get that Indicating a resigned attitude; eg 'Floods most winters. You get that.'

141

you make a better door than a window Indicating somebody is standing in your way.

you think you're a flowerpot because you've got a hole in your bum You are vain.

you wouldn't make a bus arse's horse-hole You are hopeless.

you wouldn't read about it! Exclamation of surprise or amazement.

your mother swims after troop ships You bastard, and your mother's a whore.

you're a trimmer! A curse or compliment, from 'trim', to thrash.

you're a you'rer Exasperated assessment of a mischievous child by someone lost for the right expression.

you're as full of kid as a pregnant goat You are a great teaser.

you're brave in the henhouse when the rooster's not there Bully, coward.

Zots

zack A sixpence. If something is 'not worth a zack', it is worthless.

zambuck Member of the Order of St John who gives first-aid, originating with their role at sporting fixtures attending all injuries, the word from the all-purpose ointment.

zonk Dolt; eg 'You zonk, you've spilled it everywhere.'

zoo, feeding time at the When food is served at social functions and people pig in.

zoom University drinking game based on the Hokonui swindle, which can involve Italian words and eye contacts. Roger Hall reports that at Otago University this 'game of skill' involves participants sitting in a circle going whizz/zoom/bounce, drinking each time they make a mistake.

zots Pimples, a variant of 'zit'.